THE MEANING OF KNOCK

Edited by Donal Flanagan

The Meaning of Knock

the columba press

First published in 1997 by
the columba press
55A Spruce Avenue, Stillorgan Industrial Park
Blackrock, Co Dublin

Cover by Bill Bolger
Origination by The Columba Press
Printed in Ireland by Colour Books Ltd, Dublin

ISBN 1 85607 197 9

The Illustrations
The pictures throughout this book offer a parallel story, highlighting major developments at the apparition gable from the beginning until the present day. All the picture sources were provided by Knock Shrine and the publishers gratefully acknowledge the assistance of Carmel Neary and Pat Lavelle in this matter. The pictures on pp 7 and 17 are from the Wynne collection and the photographs on pp 71 and 83, and the photograph on the front cover, were taken by Peter O'Toole of John Hinde Ltd and are used by permission.

Contents

CHAPTER I

A short history of Knock

Tom Neary

This early picture of the apparition gable shows the low stone wall over which young John Curry had to be lifted so that he could see the apparition in 1879 (see page 11).

The year 1879 was a turning point in Irish history. The famine of that year was the final one, and to solve the land troubles, Michael Davitt, a Mayo man from Straide, founded the Land League on Saturday 16 August in Daly's Hotel (now the Imperial) in Castlebar. This ray of earthly hope was to be augmented by a ray of heavenly hope in the same month – the apparition at Knock.

Prior to the apparition, the village of Knock was insignificant, consisting of a handful of thatched whitewashed cottages, inhabited by the plain, humble, hard-working people of the place. The church, small and cruciform in shape, was in the centre of the village and beside it were two small schools – one for boys and one for girls. There was a post office and a few little shops. The parochial house was a three-roomed thatched cottage similar to the other cottages. Knock was poor, peaceful and unknown, dead to the outside world. The surrounding areas were poor and the farms were small.

The parish church, erected by Fr Patrick O'Grady in 1828 and dedicated to St John the Baptist, had a tower at its northern end and a gable facing south. It replaced a thatched structure which stood on the same site and was built in the penal times. On completion, the following inscription was placed on its west outside wall: 'My house shall be called the House of Prayer to All Nations. This is the Gate of the Lord; the just shall enter into it.'

The apparition at Knock

The story of Knock as a shrine began on Thursday 21 August, 1879. The weather was fine in the morning and the local people were busy with various kinds of work. Some were saving hay. Others were drawing home turf from the bog. About midday the rain came, first in a drizzle, later in a downpour.

In a thatched cottage east of the church, Mrs Byrne, a widow, lived with her family. South-west of the church, the Parish Priest of Knock, Archdeacon Bartholomew Cavanagh, sat at the fire drying his clothes in his thatched cottage. He had been visiting a distant part of the parish on horseback and was soaked with rain on his return journey.

On the evening of 21 August, 1879, the Parish Priest's housekeeper, Mary McLoughlin (45 years), went to visit the Byrne home and when she was leaving, Mary Byrne (29 years) walked out the narrow roadway with her, chatting as they went. It joined the main road through the village near the church and a short distance south of it. Coming into view of the church gable, Mary Byrne noticed a strange and wonderful sight. She saw figures standing out from the south-facing gable wall. She thought they were statues at first, but when she noticed that they were moving, she knew they were not. Then she recognised the Blessed Virgin Mary. It was then about 8 pm.

Filled with excitement, she dashed back to her home and summoned the other members of the household – her mother Margaret (68 years), her brother Dominick Junior (18 to 20 years), her sister Margaret (21 years) and her grand-daughter Catherine Murray (8¾ years).

Dominick Junior alerted Patrick Hill (11 years), a nephew of Mrs Byrne. He lived in Claremorris but was at the Byrne home that day and was bringing turf from the bog with a donkey. He also alerted his cousin, Dominick Byrne Senior (36 years), John Durkan (about 24 years), John Curry (5½ years) and Patrick Byrne (16 years).

Mary Byrne also called out Judith Campbell (22 years), who lived across the road from the church, and Bridget Trench or Bríd Ní Thrinsigh as she was known in Irish (74 to 75 years), who was in the Campbell cottage when she arrived with the wondrous news.

Mrs Hugh Flatley (44 years) saw the apparition as she was passing by the church on the main road. Patrick Walsh (about 65 years) saw the light of the apparition as he was going through his land, a half mile from the church.

What did the witnesses see on that wet Thursday evening of 21 August, 1879?

They distinctly beheld the Blessed Virgin Mary, life-size, standing about two feet or so above the ground, clothed in white robes which were fastened at the neck. Her hands were raised to the level of the shoulders, with the palms facing one another and slanting inwards towards the face. She appeared to be praying. Her eyes were turned towards heaven. She wore a brilliant golden crown on her head and, over the forehead where the crown fitted the brow, a beautiful golden rose. The upper parts of the crown appeared to be a series of sparkles or glittering crosses. Our Lady's feet and ankles were visible. One foot – the right – was slightly in advance of the other. She did not speak.

Our witnesses saw St Joseph to the Blessed Virgin's right hand. His head was bent from the shoulders forward. He appeared to be paying his respects. His hands were joined. There was a line or dark mearing between the figure of the Blessed Virgin and the spot where he stood. His robes were white but they did not cover his feet. He appeared to be aged, with grey whiskers and greyish hair. He did not speak.

St John the Evangelist was on Our Lady's left. He was dressed like a bishop. On his head was a small mitre. In his left hand was a Missal or Book of Gospels. It lay open and the witnesses saw the lines and the letters in the book. He appeared to be preaching. His right hand was raised to the height of the head. The index finger and the middle finger were raised. The other three fingers were shut. His feet were visible. He did not speak.

St John's left hand was turned towards an altar that was beside him and directly under the window in the centre of the gable. The altar was plain and white. On the altar stood a lamb – the size of a lamb about eight weeks old. The lamb was facing the western sky. Behind the lamb, a large cross stood erect on the altar. The witnesses saw angels hovering around the lamb during the whole time. They saw their wings fluttering but they did not perceive their heads or faces which were not turned towards them.

At times, all the figures moved out from the gable and, at other times, receded again, especially when approached. Apparently, the movement of the figures and the angels was for the purpose of at-tracting the attention of the onlookers. The figures were full and round, life-size and life-like.

It was daylight when the apparition was first seen, but shortly afterwards darkness fell. A striking aspect of the apparition was the extraordinary light which did not resemble any light ever seen by the witnesses. It was exceedingly brilliant and covered most of the gable from the ground up to the window and higher.

In 1879, there was a meadow by the southern gable and the figures were standing on top of the grass. A low stone wall ran along by the narrow roadway parallel to the gable. Patrick Hill had to lift up little John Curry to see the apparition as he was not tall enough to see over the top of the wall. These two children went up very close to the figures and Patrick looked into the book in St John's hand and saw the writing in it.

The witnesses reacted in various ways to what they saw. Some shed tears. Others prayed the Rosary. They experienced joy and delight.

For the duration of the apparition, the witnesses were under the pouring rain which was driven in the direction of the church gable by a strong southerly wind. They were very wet but they noticed that the rain did not fall within the area of the light, on the figures or the part of the gable where the apparition was. Bridget Trench felt the ground carefully with her hands and it was perfectly dry. The ordinary laws of nature, it would seem, were suspended. This was the miracle that accompanied the apparition.

Judith Campbell left the scene to attend to her sick mother but found her in a swoon at her cottage door. She had heard the news that had been brought to her house and had made an attempt to go to the church gable. Judith ran back to the gable and asked for assistance. Those who were there rushed to the aid of her mother but returned hurriedly. On their arrival at the gable, there was no apparition to be seen. The rain was dashing on the gable wall and all was in darkness.

Early reactions to the apparition

Knock, in Gaelic 'Cnoc' meaning 'Hill', would never be the same again. This great happening changed its name from 'Cnoc' to 'Cnoc Mhuire' – 'Mary's Hill'.

Archdeacon Cavanagh, the Parish Priest of Knock, did not see the apparition though his housekeeper told him about it and said that it would be worth his while to go to the church gable. He did not go and regretted his decision for the rest of his life.

The Archdeacon was known, far and wide, for the sanctity of his life and his great love for the poor, to whom he gave all his possessions. He had lived and worked through the Great Famine in Westport prior to his appointment to Knock/Aghamore in 1867. He kept a diary in which he recorded hundreds of extraordinary or miraculous cures that occurred at Knock in the years following the apparition. Cures, of course, have continued down the years to the present.

When news of the apparition spread, thousands of pilgrims flocked to Knock bringing with them their sick. The first recorded cure took place ten days after the apparition. A twelve-year-old girl named Delia Gordon was cured of deafness while attending Mass in Knock, when her mother placed cement from the apparition gable in her ear.

In a short time the gable was stripped of its cement by the pilgrims and it had to be protected by a covering of boards. Later, the whole gable was given a fresh coat of cement and the boarding, on which there were racks for holding crutches, was also replaced. In September, 1880, a statue of Our Lady of Knock was erected on the spot where the Blessed Virgin stood and, shortly afterwards, a protective iron railing was erected in front of the gable.

The first commission

Archbishop John Mac Hale of Tuam set up a commission of priests to enquire into the reported apparition in October, 1879. All fifteen witnesses were examined and the commission, in their report to the archbishop, stated that the testimony of all, taken as a whole, was trustworthy and satisfactory.

Despite the findings of the commission, Knock had to fight very vigorous opposition and criticism of a destructive kind. The whole story was subjected to the most scientific examination by competent lay and clerical critics. However, no adequate natural explanation of the apparition could be found.

As news of the apparition spread, people flocked to Knock, often bringing the sick with them. Many left their sticks and crutches at the gable, and this picture shows clearly the effect of the practice of scratching the cement from the gable wall (see page 50). The sign in the picture reads 'It is important that any miraculous cures wrought here would be made known to the parish priest.'

The first pilgrimages

The first organised pilgrimage to visit Knock came from Limerick in March 1880. It was the Archconfraternity of the Holy Family, attached to the Redemptorists' church there. The Archbishop of Tuam, Dr John MacHale, received a deputation from this pilgrimage in his residence, spoke words of encouragement to them, blessed them and their families, and said in reference to the pilgrimage: 'It is a great blessing to the poor people of the West, in their wretchedness and misery and suffering, that the Blessed Virgin Mother of God has appeared among them.' This statement, which was published in the press of the day, shows clearly that the archbishop had accepted the findings of the 1879 commission and that he believed in the apparition.

On the first anniversary of the apparition, Saturday 21 August, 1880, Knock was crowded with pilgrims. They arrived in sidecars, cabs, waggonettes, donkey carts and many came on foot. On that evening, four thousand pilgrims took part in a candlelight procession around the Church of the Apparition.

A visitor to Knock in 1881 was the internationally known Sr Mary Francis Clare Cusack, the Nun of Kenmare. This noted writer, well ahead of her time in many respects, had plans to build a convent in Knock. It was only partly completed when she had some disagreement with the authorities. As a result, she left Knock and the building was never finished. She claimed in her autobiography to have been cured at the shrine, and in 1882 had a book published by P. J. Kennedy, New York, entitled *Three Visits to Knock*.

In 1882, Archbishop Lynch of Toronto, Canada, visited Knock in thanksgiving for a cure, and presented a hand-embroidered banner to the shrine bearing the words 'Toronto Grateful'. Around the same time, Archbishop Clune of Perth, Australia, came to Knock for the same purpose and gave an oil painting of St Joseph and the Child Jesus to the shrine. In 1883, Archbishop Murphy of Hobart, Tasmania, had his sight completely restored in Knock. His gift to the shrine was a large oil painting of the apparition.

On the feast of the Immaculate Conception, 8 December, 1897, Archdeacon Cavanagh died in the hostel now known as St Mary's, which he had built for pilgrims and retreatants. It passed to the Sisters of Charity of St Vincent de Paul around 1930. The room in which he died is now the convent chapel. He was laid to rest within the Church of the Apparition in the western transept.

Pilgrims came to Knock in their thousands from all parts in the twenty-five years following the apparition, but in the next quarter century there was a temporary decline in numbers. This period included the years of World War I.

In the early decades, the main pilgrimage days were the feasts of Our Lady and the largest crowds were always present on 15 August, the occasion of an annual national pilgrimage to Knock. All-night vigils were also held on the eves of the feasts. Many pilgrims walked to the shrine barefoot on rough gravel roads and performed the station at the shrine on their bare knees.

A new phase

A new phase began for Knock shrine in 1926. Archbishop Gilmartin of Tuam approved a formula of devotions for pilgrimages at the request of Fr Tuffy.

The Golden Jubilee of the Knock apparition was celebrated at the shrine on Sunday 18 August, 1929. This was a truly historic occasion, for present at the ceremonies was Dr Thomas P. Gilmartin, Archbishop of Tuam. He was making his first visit to Knock shrine and this was the first time any archbishop of the archdiocese had participated in pilgrimage ceremonies.

In 1935 a medical bureau was established at Knock in order to help the ecclesiastical authorities to investigate the claims to miraculous cures.

Knock Shrine Society

On 21 August, 1935, Knock Shrine Society of Handmaids, Stewards and Promoters was founded by William D. Coyne and his wife, J. C. Coyne. Composed of lay people, it had as its first patron,

Archbishop Gilmartin. At the inaugural meeting in the old school in Knock, a mere handful of the laity was present. Today, there are more than twelve hundred members in the society. Down the years they have promoted Knock shrine in various ways and, to this day, care for the sick, maintain order in the grounds and buildings and participate in the liturgical ceremonies A voluntary body, it has people from all parts of Ireland and from all age groups. A more recent addition has been the Pious Union of Handmaids who devote their lives to the care of the sick in a special way. They are consecrated handmaids who take vows.

The second commission

In 1936, Archbishop Gilmartin established a second commission to interview the three witnesses to the apparition who were still alive, namely, Mary Byrne, then Mrs Mary O'Connell, Patrick Byrne and John Curry. The Byrnes, interviewed in their homes in Knock, confirmed the evidence they gave to the first commission in 1879. John Curry was examined in New York before a special tribunal set up there by the Archbishop of New York, Cardinal Hayes, on 6 July, 1937. He was then living in one of the Homes of the Little Sisters of the Poor. The verdict of this second commission, which took three years to complete its work, was that the evidence of the witnesses was upright and trustworthy.

Mrs Mary O'Connell (nee Mary Byrne) died on 19 October, 1936, at the age of eighty-six – the principal witness to Knock apparition.

In 1937, no less than eighty thousand pilgrims visited Knock and of that number, fifty-eight thousand came on Sundays. Figures for attendance in 1938 were one hundred and twenty thousand, of which seventy-two thousand came on Sundays.

The first edition of *Knock Shrine Annual* was published early in 1938 by Knock Shrine Society.

On Sunday 1 May, 1938, outdoor Stations of the Cross – a gift from Knock Shrine Society – were blessed in Knock by the Auxiliary Bishop of Tuam, Dr Joseph Walsh. That same year, Red Cross huts were erected opposite the front door of the Apparition Church.

The gable was sheeted with wood to prevent the removal of cement and there were racks for hanging crutches and sticks. The man on the ladder is intent on getting cement from above the sheeting. By this time a small shrine had been added.

They were the very first facilities provided for the sick in Knock, and in 1939 another shelter was provided for pilgrims and invalids south of the apparition gable. It was affectionately known as 'The Green Shed'.

The greatest pilgrimage occasion in 1939 was on Sunday, 20 August, when Knock Shrine celebrated its Diamond Jubilee in glorious sunshine. A beautiful new processional statue of Our Lady of Knock was blessed by Canon Grealy, in the presence of the Shrine Stewards, on Diamond Jubilee Day and was then carried, for the first time, at the head of the Rosary Procession by men from the thirty-two counties of Ireland, in dark suits and blue sashes, boy scouts from Armagh forming a guard of honour for the statue.

On Sunday 17 September, 1939, there were twenty thousand children in Knock, praying for world peace, and, in all, one hundred and seventy thousand pilgrims visited the shrine in that year, which saw the passing of Archbishop Gilmartin on 14 October.

Developments in the forties

A new Oratory was blessed and dedicated to Our Lady of the Assumption at the apparition gable on Sunday 5 May, 1940, by the Archbishop of Tuam, Dr Joseph Walsh.

On Sunday 18 August, 1940, a great national peace pilgrimage was held in the first year of World War II, when ten thousand Masses were offered all over Ireland in honour of Our Lady of Knock and the ten thousand Mass Cards were placed at the shrine.

The last surviving witness of the Knock apparition living in the village, Patrick Byrne, died on 29 April, 1943 at the age of eighty. He was buried in Knock cemetery where most of the witnesses lie at rest. John Curry is buried in New York, Patrick Hill in Boston, and Catherine Murray in the neighbouring parish of Bekan.

The outstanding event of 1945 was the national pilgrimage of thanksgiving to God for sparing Ireland from the horrors of the World War. It was held on 19 August, the Sunday on which Knock Shrine Society presented as a thanksgiving gift, beautiful hand-embroidered vestments made by the Benedictine Nuns of Kylemore Abbey, Connemara.

Fr Patrick J. Peyton, CSC, the American Radio Priest and a native of Co Mayo, held a Rosary Rally at Knock on Sunday 18 August, 1946. Knock Shrine Rosary Crusade was formally announced in Knock on Sunday 18 May, 1947, when Fr James Horan, CC, Aghamore, addressed the pilgrims during the public ceremonies in the afternoon.

One million pilgrims came to Knock in 1954 – The Marian Year – despite very mixed weather.

Thirteen trains, fleets of buses and private cars took twenty-five thousand children – many of them invalids – to Knock on Sunday 9 May, 1954, on the National Children's Pilgrimage.

The greatest single pilgrimage of the Marian Year, and the largest in the shrine's seventy-five year history, was the National Pioneer Total Abstinence Association Pilgrimage when fifty thousand pilgrims were present. They came in twenty-two trains, four hundred and four buses, seven thousand cars, on bicycles and many walked. The date was Sunday 19 September, 1954.

On Monday 1 November, 1954, Pope Pius XII proclaimed the new feast of Our Lady, Queen, and solemnly crowned the picture of Our Lady and Child, *Salus Populi Romani*, in St Peter's, Rome. Over four hundred Marian shrines were represented at the ceremony, amongst them thirty-six Handmaids and Stewards from Knock.

On Wednesday 8 December, 1954, the Processional Statue of Our Lady of Knock was solemnly crowned in the Church of the Apparition in Knock.

The eucharistic blessing of the sick took place for the first time in Knock on Sunday 29 April, 1956.

A Silver Jubilee

Celebrations marking the Silver Jubilee of Knock Shrine Society were held on 25 and 26 June, 1960. Pope John XXIII sent his Apostolic Blessing and letters of congratulation were received from church dignitaries all over the world. The Society presented the shrine with the Knock monstrance, which is used for the eucharistic blessing of the sick.

What have become known as the Last Thursday Ceremonies for the Sick, began on the last Thursday in May, 1961, and have continued to the present day. Sodalities for the invalids include 'The Volunteers of Suffering' and 'Helpers of the Sick'.

A beautiful stained-glass window was blessed and unveiled in Knock church on Sunday 27 August, 1961, in memory of Fr J. A. Rabbitte, O Carm, Whitefriar St, Dublin. Cured at Knock in his youth, he organised the first Carmelite pilgrimage to Knock and led the subsequent pilgrimages until his death. The window, made by Harry Clarke Studios, Dublin, depicts Our Lady of Mount Carmel presenting the Brown Scapular to St Simon Stock.

James Horan

In 1963, an energetic, progressive priest was appointed to Knock as curate. He was Fr James Horan. For the following twenty-three years he would work to transform Knock completely, construct a basilica, arrange a papal visit and build an international airport.

At the end of the third session of the Second Vatican Council, Pope Paul vi celebrated Mass in St Peter's Basilica with the custodians of the most famous Marian shrines in the world. The date was Saturday 21 November, 1964, Feast of Our Lady's Presentation. The Archbishop of Tuam, Dr Walsh, represented Knock.

The foundation stone for an Invalids' Rest House was blessed and laid by Archbishop Walsh, on Thursday 22 August, 1968. In that year also, the Processional Square was developed to accommodate large pilgrimages in the open.

Knock Marriage Introductions Bureau, authorised by the bishops of Connacht, was established in 1968, under the patronage of Our Lady of Knock.

Dr Joseph Cunnane – a native son of Knock – was consecrated Archbishop of Tuam on Tuesday 17 March, 1969. There was great rejoicing in Knock parish and at the shrine on that day.

On Sunday 3 May, 1970, Archbishop Cunnane announced in Knock that, in co-operation with the priests connected with Knock shrine and the Knock Shrine Society, he had under consideration a plan for the provision of a church at Knock that he hoped would be a fitting memorial for the celebration of the centenary of the apparition in 1979. On Saturday 4 July, 1970, a Votive Mass in honour of Our Lady of Knock was celebrated for the first time at Knock shrine.

The new St Joseph's Rest Home, a residential hostel for invalids, was opened for use during the 1971 pilgrimage season and was staffed by the Consecrated Handmaids of Our Lady of Knock. On Sunday 5 September of the same year, the Communal Anointing of the Sick was administered to the invalids for the first time.

From Sunday 6 May, 1973, the privilege of receiving Holy Communion twice in the day, on the occasion of a pilgrimage to Knock, on certain conditions, was granted.

The first Folk Museum was officially opened by Archbishop Cunnane on Tuesday 31 July, 1973, on the site of Archdeacon Cavanagh's cottage.

On the feast of All the Irish Saints, Tuesday 6 November, 1973, the site for the great new church was blessed and the first sod was turned by Archbishop Cunnane.

In 1974, the Knock Shrine Calvary was erected on the hill south of the apparition gable, consisting of fourteen white wooden crosses.

The foundation stone of the great new church was laid by Archbishop Cunnane on Thursday 15 August, 1974.

On Saturday 20 September, 1975, the first ordinations took place at Knock. On a sunny day of blue skies, seven young men of the Divine Word Missionaries, Donamon Castle, Co Roscommon, were ordained priests by Archbishop Cunnane in an outdoor ceremony.

The ninety-six feet bronze spire for the new church was hoisted into position on the Feast of the Holy Rosary, Tuesday 7 October, 1975.

The new church was blessed and dedicated on Sunday 18 July, 1976, by Archbishop Cunnane, assisted by Archbishop Ryan of Dublin and Archbishop Morris of Cashel and Emly, in the presence of Cardinal Conway and the bishops of Ireland.

Standing on the site of the Byrne cottage, where five of the apparition witnesses lived, the new church, later to be given the status of Basilica, is circular in shape, is divided into five chapels and can accommodate ten thousand pilgrims. It covers more than an acre of ground. Its national features include a pillar of stone from each of the thirty-two counties of Ireland supporting the ambulatory, and replicas of Irish medieval church windows from each of the four provinces, in the main radiating walls, separating the chapels. The altar is in the centre of the hexagonal sanctuary and behind it is the Blessed Sacrament Chapel. Louis J. Brennan & Associates, in association with Daithi P. Hanly, Dublin, were the architects. The general contractors were John Paul & Co, Dublin.

21 July, 1977, Archbishop Cunnane laid the founda-
of the Rest-and-Care Centre for one-day invalids.
John's, it was blessed and opened by the archbishop on
3 February, 1978.

The first National Public Novena in honour of Our Lady of Knock
took place from 14 to 22 August, 1977, and the novena themes were
the familiar titles of Our Lady. It has continued, in unbroken se-
quence, to this day.

The first centenary

There was feverish activity in Knock in 1978 as many things were
being put in place for the centenary celebrations the following year.
Work began on the erection of a Confessional Chapel and, towards
the end of the year, work commenced on the construction of an
Oratory and the erection of new shrine statuary at the apparition
gable. A Religious Vocations' Centre was opened in Knock on
Sunday 7 May, 1978.

The Centenary Year, 1979, was a truly memorable one, in many respects. The new Church of Our Lady Queen of Ireland was consecrated on Sunday 25 March, Feast of the Annunciation, and by the
end of the year, between two and three million pilgrims had visited
Knock.

The special ceremonies marking the centenary of the apparition
were held on the 15 August, 1979, and were attended by church and
state dignitaries, including many cardinals and the President of
Ireland, Dr Patrick Hillery.

The Papal Visit

The event which overshadowed all other events in 1979, was the
Papal Visit. On Sunday 30 September, Pope John Paul II came as a
pilgrim to Knock shrine – the goal of his journey to Ireland. He was
welcomed on his arrival by helicopter, by Archbishop Cunnane and
Mgr James Horan.

After the Holy Father had walked along the roof of the ambulatory
of the new church, on the south side, in full view of the crowds, he

entered the church and addressed two thousand five hundred invalids, laid his hands on them and blessed them. Then followed his
address to the Handmaids, Stewards and the Directors of Pilgrimages
of Cnoc Mhuire.

The Pope then celebrated Mass at a specially constructed altar out-
doors, between the new church and the apparition gable, the cen-
trepiece of which was a replica of the Celtic High Cross of Ahinney.
Concelebrating with him was Cardinal Tomás Ó Fiaich, Archbishop
Cunnane, Mgr James Horan, and the bishops of Ireland.

During the Mass, the Holy Father delivered a long homily which
ended with a beautiful Act of Consecration of Ireland and the Irish
people to Mary Mother of the Church. He also gave the Anointing
of the Sick to a small number of invalids.

After Mass, Pope John Paul raised the new Church of Our Lady
Queen of Ireland to the status of Basilica, to honour Our Lady of
Knock in her centenary year. He also presented as his own personal
tribute and gift to the shrine of Knock, a rose in gold and a large or-
nate candle.

He then travelled in an open car or 'popemobile' to the Apparition
Chapel and knelt in silent prayer. He lit a candle to Family Prayer
to stress its importance in the home, at the apparition gable wall.

Knock Airport

On 25 September, 1980, the government gave approval in principle
for the construction of Knock airport. Outline planning permission was given on 3 December, 1980, and the cutting of the first sod
took place on 2 May, 1981. The airport was officially opened by
Charles Haughey, TD, on Friday 30 May, 1986.

Most welcome arrivals in Knock in the Autumn of 1981 were the
enclosed Carmelite Sisters, to begin a new phase of life in their con-
vent/monastery, Tranquilla, overlooking the shrine. Their official
arrival was marked by the dedication of their chapel to Mary, on
Thursday 15 October, 1981.

In 1983 a spacious Blessed Sacrament Chapel was opened for daily adoration. Unusual in its design, it gives the impression of rising up out of the ground and ascending heavenwards, in three distinct sections.

St Brigid's Hostel for retired Handmaids and invalids was brought into use in 1984.

On Friday 1 August, 1986, Mgr James Horan died suddenly in Lourdes where he was leading a pilgrimage. His body was flown from Tarbes airport near Lourdes to Knock, the first funeral at the airport. Thousands attended the arrival of his remains and funeral Mass in Knock Basilica on Tuesday 5 August. He was laid to rest at the rear of the Basilica where his grave is constantly visited by the ordinary and the great. This wonder worker, builder of the modern Knock, had rare talents, charisma and the common touch. May he rest in peace.

In 1987, the new Folk Museum was opened in the shrine grounds. It portrays life in rural Ireland at the time of the apparition and after, shrine history and the achievements of Mgr James Horan.

In the Spring of 1988, the fiftieth edition of *Knock Shrine Annual* was published. This yearly record of events at Knock has been edited by the same person, Mrs J.C. Coyne, for fifty years, since it first appeared in 1938.

The ceremony of dedication of the new Chapel of Reconciliation took place on 15 July, 1990. The chief celebrant was Dr Joseph Cassidy, Archbishop of Tuam, and the Presiding Prelate was Archbishop Emmanuele Gerada, Apostolic Nuncio to Ireland.

The new Apparition Chapel was formally dedicated by Archbishop Cassidy on Sunday 10 May, 1992. It frames the apparition gable, with its magnificent white marble statuary representing the apparition scene as described by the witnesses. It was designed and carved in Rome by Professor Ferri. This most functional, inventive and imaginative building in stone, steel, woodwork and glass, had as its architect the Polish-born Andrzej Wejchert.

The first Episcopal Ordination in Knock took place in the Basilica on Sunday 13 September, 1992, when the Right Rev Michael Neary became Titular Bishop of Quaestoriana and Auxiliary to the

Archbishop of Tuam. When Dr Cassidy resigned for health reasons in 1995, Bishop Neary became Archbishop of Tuam. His family has had a long association with Knock.

Mother Teresa of Calcutta visited Knock on Saturday 5 June, 1993, where she was greeted by fifty thousand pilgrims on a glorious sunny day. After she had prayed in the Apparition Chapel, she was driven through the crowds to the Basilica where she was formally welcomed by Mgr Grealy. Having addressed the thousands of invalids in the Basilica, she recited her 'Rosary for Life' from the outdoor altar in the Basilica tower, and then attended Mass there, during which Archbishop Cassidy paid her a special tribute.

Knock Shrine Society celebrated its Diamond Jubilee on Sunday 27 August, 1995, when ceremonies marking the event were held in Knock Basilica. Present at the ceremonies was Mrs J.C. Coyne who, with her husband, founded the Society in 1935. She received a Blessing from Pope John Paul 11 and a Scroll of Tribute from the Handmaids and Stewards.

New chapels, a Guided Prayer Centre with audio-visual room and youth facilities, a Religious Books Centre, a housing scheme for the elderly, together with landscaping, lawns, gardens and flower beds, added in recent years, make Knock's spacious domain an oasis of peace and loveliness.

The inscription placed on the western wall of the old Knock church, over half a century prior to the apparition, is still there today. In the light of all that has happened between 1879 and 1996 – a span of 117 years – it is truly prophetic. Knock has become the 'House of Prayer to All Nations' and the 'Gate of the Lord'.

CHAPTER 2

The apparition and its meaning

Donal Flanagan

In the autumn of 1880 the apparition gable was given a new coat of cement and an iron railing was erected for protection. A statue of Our Lady of Knock was placed inside the railing.

There were fifteen witnesses to the apparition at Knock on the evening of 21 August, 1879. They were examined by a commission set up by Archbishop McHale following the apparition. Their statements about what they saw agree substantially. The commission's verdict was that the group were credible witnesses and that it was reasonable to accept their story.

This judgment was repeated by the second commission which sat in 1936. The three surviving witnesses were examined again under oath. They gave accounts of the events at Knock in 1879 similar to those they had given more than fifty years before. Fr James Fergus (later Bishop of Achonry) was official secretary to the 1936 commission. He noted at the time that the judges believed that the witnesses spoke the truth sincerely and that the manner in which the evidence was given had all the appearances of sincerity.

> All the witnesses were straightforward, evidently sincere, not anxious to make a point. It appears to us certain that the witnesses did see something objective at the gable of Knock Church on 21 August 1879. Considering that there were so many witnesses of various kinds and ages, men and women, boys, girls and even children, and that the alleged apparition was seen for so long a time, it seems to us very unlikely that the witnesses were the victims of an ocular delusion.

Talking to a journalist in 1978, the then Bishop Fergus said again: 'I don't think that, on the evidence, you could possibly explain Knock as being an illusion. Something certainly happened on that occasion.' And he added, very significantly: 'I'm very slow to believe anything like that. I'm not a bit credulous. But it is very hard to see how the apparition could have been seen unless something real happened.'

The three surviving witnesses

Three witnesses who gave evidence to the original commission survived to give evidence again in 1936. They were Mary O'Connell (formerly Byrne), Patrick Byrne and John Curry. Their evidence in 1936 was practically the same as their earlier depositions. The agreement of all the witnesses, and the fact that there was no withdrawal of their reports by any one of them, is significant. Mary O'Connell, in fact, provided in the last year of her life, a sworn statement before a Commissioner for Oaths. The final words of this statement, made in January 1936, are striking. They are: 'I am clear about everything I have said and I make this statement knowing I am going before my God.' She died on 19 October that year at the age of eighty-six.

Mary O'Connell's original statement is worth examining in some detail. It was taken by the three priests who had been appointed by Archbishop John McHale to look into the reported apparition and to investigate its genuineness. They were the Parish Priests of Knock, of Ballyhaunis and of Claremorris (Kilcolman), Archdeacon Cavanagh, Canon James Waldron and Canon Ulick Bourke. They chose to take evidence from a selection of witnesses, fifteen in all. They reported that the testimony of these witnesses, taken as a whole, was trustworthy and satisfactory. The depositions of the witnesses were recorded at the Catholic church at Knock on 8 October 1879.

When Mary Byrne (later O'Connell) gave her evidence in 1879 she was a young woman, twenty-nine years of age. Her statement is simple and plainly expressed.

> I beheld three figures standing out from the gable rather to the west side of it and a little out from the wall and at a height of about one and a half or two feet from the ground. The figure of the Blessed Virgin appeared to be larger than that of St Joseph or of the episcopal figure having the mitre on his head and the book of Gospels on his left hand … the third figure appeared to me to be that of St John the Evangelist.

Mary Byrne points out carefully that her identification of St John was less certain than her identification of the other two figures and was based on what she calls in her evidence 'a surmise'. It was a conjecture based on a similarity which she noticed between the episcopal figure in the apparition and a statue she had seen in the chapel at Lecanvey, near Westport.

She continues:

> The saint (i.e. St John) appeared to me to look to the altar which
> stood … towards the centre of the gable and under the window.
> The altar appeared to me to be a large full-sized altar … It had
> no candles or linens nor any ornamentation … but above the
> altar and resting on it was a lamb with its face towards St John
> … I remained from half past eight o'clock … I went away at
> half past nine o'clock to see Mrs Campbell who was ailing and
> whose death was expected. After twenty minutes or so I re-
> turned and came by the chapel gable. The vision had by this
> time vanished. The place was quite dark.

A message?

People sometimes tend to regard the apparition at Knock as peculiar
among Marian apparitions because none of the visionaries received a
verbal message from the Blessed Virgin. This fact does not make
Knock unique among Marian apparitions, for in the apparition at
Portmain in France, on 17 January 1871, Our Lady did not speak
either. At Portmain, however, the children were able to read the written
messages which surrounded the apparition and invited them to pray,
with the promise that God would soon answer them. Portmain, with
its message written in the sky, is different from Knock with its silent
figures. At Knock there was neither a verbal nor a written message
but this does not appear to have disturbed the visionaries.

Catherine Rynne notes in her fine book, *Knock 1879-1979* (Dublin,
Veritas, 1979), 'Much has been made of the fact that no words were
spoken at Knock and this poses an obstacle to belief for some' (p
148). She recalls the wise words of the very distinguished Capuchin
scholar, Fr James, who wrote: 'There are times, even in this world
of space and time, when language fails us and silence is our only adequate means of communication.'

Among the visionaries, Patrick Hill, then a young boy of eleven,
comments in his evidence on the silence of the apparition.

> The figures were full and round as if they had a body and life;
> they said nothing.

Others who saw the apparition make no comment on the silence and do not seem to be in any way disturbed by it. Thus Bríd Ní Thrinsigh (Brigid Trench), who gave her evidence in Irish, makes an allusion to the figures not speaking. She was happy that the Blessed Virgin had visited Knock and thankful to God for this great favour. Describing her approach to the place of the apparition she said:

> Nuair a shroicheas an áit sin chonaiceas go soiléir na trí figiúirí. Chaitheas mé féin síos ar mo ghlúna agus gháireas: 'Céad míle buíochas le Dia agus leis an Maighdin ghlórmhair a thug dúinn an teaspeánadh seo.'
>
> (When I reached the place I clearly saw the three figures. I threw myself on my knees and exclaimed: 'A hundred thousand thanks to God and to the glorious Virgin who have given us this manifestation.')

She added at another point in her statement:

> D'fhánas ansin uair a chloig ar fad agus nuair a thángas ansin i dtosach cheapas nach bhfágfainn an áit go deo. Leanas ag athrá na Coróine Mhuire ar mo phaidrín fad a bhíos ansin agus mhothaíos an-aoibhneas agus pléisiúr is mé ag féachaint ar an Maighdin Bheannaithe. Ní rabhas in ann smaoineamh ar thada fad a bhíos ansin ach ag tabhairt buíochais le Dia ag athrá mo phaidreacha.
>
> (I remained there for about an hour and when I came there first I thought I would never leave it. I continued to repeat the Rosary on my beads while there and I felt great delight and pleasure in looking at the Blessed Virgin. I could think of nothing else while there but giving thanks to God repeating my prayers.)

Bríd left the apparition site expecting to return to see the figures again. She reports her deep disappointment.

> Ní rachainn comh túisce is a chuas ach mhacnaíos go leanfadh na figiúirí agus an ghile sin ansin i gcónaí agus ar theacht arais dom go bhfeicfinn arís iad.
>
> (I would not have gone so soon as I did but that I thought the

figures and the brightness would remain there always and that I would see them again on my return.)

Other witnesses went away and expressed the same disappointment at finding the vision gone on their return. The fact that none of the three figures spoke or gave any message does not seem to have disturbed any of these visionaries. They seem to have accepted the apparition with great simplicity as a gift from God.

The themes of joy, happiness, gratefulness to God, are sounded by several witnesses besides Bríd Ní Thrinsigh. Thus Dominic Byrne, brother of Mary O'Connell (nee Byrne), who was about twenty years old, reported:

> I was filled with admiration at the sight I saw. I was so affected I shed tears on the occasion. I continued there looking on for fully an hour.

There is a general absence in the testimonies of any element of complaint that there was no verbal message given by the figures. The chief emotions felt by the group were joy, happiness and a sense of gratitude to God. In fact, the absence of a verbal message may well have freed the witnesses for the task of describing the vision and its various figures with some exactness.

The Blessed Virgin

The female figure in the apparition was described in some detail by the witnesses and clearly identified as the Blessed Virgin. There seems to have been no hesitation on this point. Bríd Ní Thrinsigh reported:

> Bhí an Mhaighdean Bheannaithe i lár báire; bhí culaith gheal uirthi agus bhí sí clúdaithe i mball éadaigh bháin amháin, de réir dealraimh; bhí a lámha ardaithe go dtí an suíomh céanna in a mbíonn lámha sagairt nuair a bhíonn sé ag guí ag Aifreann naofa. Shonraíos go gléineach codanna íochtaracha a cos, agus phógas iad trí huaire; bhí rud éigin ar a ceann cosúil le coróin agus bhí a súile ardaithe i dtreo na nimhe. Bhíos comh tógtha leis an Maighdin Bheannaithe nár thugas mórán aire d'éinne eile. Mar sin féin chonaiceas chomh maith an dá fhigiúr eile …

(The Blessed Virgin was in the centre; she was clothed in white and covered with what appeared to be one white gamment; her hands were raised to the same position as that in which a priest holds his hands when praying at Holy Mass. I remarked distinctly the lower portions of her feet and kissed them three times; she had on her head something resembling a crown and her eyes were turned up heavenwards. I was so taken with the Blessed Virgin that I did not pay much attention to any other, yet I saw also the two other figures ...)

Mary Byrne (later O'Connell) said in her description:

The Virgin stood erect with eyes raised to heaven, her hands elevated to the shoulders or a little higher, the palms inclined slightly towards the shoulders or bosom. She wore a large cloak of a white colour hanging in full folds and somewhat loosely around her shoulders and fastened to the neck. She wore a crown on the head, rather a large crown, and it appeared to me somewhat yellower than the dress or robes worn by Our Blessed Lady.

A further witness, Patrick Hill, a young boy, eleven years old, told the 1879 Commission of Enquiry:

I distinctly beheld the Blessed Virgin Mary, life-size, standing about two feet or so above the ground, clothed in white robes which were fastened at the neck. Her hands were raised to the height of the shoulders, as if in prayer, with the palms facing one another but slanting inwards towards the face. The palms were not turned towards the people but facing each other as I have described. She appeared to be praying. Her eyes were turned as I saw towards heaven. She wore a brilliant crown on her head and over the forehead where the crown fitted the brow, a beautiful rose. The crown appeared brilliant and of a golden brightness, of a deeper hue, inclined to a mellow yellow than the striking whiteness of the robes she wore. The upper parts of the crown appeared to be a series of sparkles or glittering crosses.

St Joseph

Just as the witnesses had neither doubt nor difficulty in identifying the central figure of the three in the apparition grouping as the Blessed Virgin, so they showed no hesitation in identifying another figure in the tableau as St Joseph. Patrick Hill declared:

> I saw St Joseph to the Blessed Virgin's right hand. His head was bent from the shoulders forward. He appeared to be paying his respects. I noticed his whiskers. They appeared slightly grey.

Mary Byrne's evidence is similar:

> In the figure of St Joseph the head was slightly bent and inclined towards the Blessed Virgin as if paying her respect. It represented the saint as somewhat aged, with grey whiskers and greyish hair.

Bríd Ní Thrinsigh mentions in her evidence that she was much taken up with the figure of Mary. Nonetheless, she insists, with some precision:

> Mar sin féin, chonaiceas chomh maith an dá fhigiúr eile, Naomh Iosaf ina sheasamh ar dheis na Maighdine Beannaithe nó ar clé mar a d'fhéachas féin air, a cheann claonta in a treo agus a lámha i gcomhar, agus an figiúir eile a thógas mar Naomh Eoin, an Soiscéalaí, bhí sé ina sheasamh ar a clé. Chualas na daoine thart timpeall orm ag rá gurbh é íomhá Naoimh Eoin é.

> (Nonetheless I saw as well the two other figures, St Joseph, standing to the right of the Blessed Virgin or to the left, as I looked at him, his head bent towards her and his hands joined. The other figure, which I took to be St John the Evangelist, was standing at her left. I heard those around me say that the image was St John.)

As with the Blessed Virgin, so with St Joseph, the various witnesses appear to have had no difficulty whatever in coming each one to a personal conclusion as to his identity. They did not need help from anyone else in making a clear identification of the Blessed Virgin and St Joseph. The same thing is not true of the third figure.

The third figure

'The third figure that stood before me', Patrick Hill (11) said in his deposition, 'was that of St John the Evangelist.' Earlier in the same statement he uses a simpler and more direct way of speaking of Our Lady and St Joseph. 'I distinctly beheld the Blessed Virgin Mary' and 'I saw St Joseph to the Blessed Virgin's right hand ...' We would perhaps expect him to say: 'I saw St John the Evangelist ...' or to use some similar formula if he had recognised the figure with the same immediacy as he had recognised Our Lady and St Joseph.

Several of the witnesses, who apparently had no problems in immediately naming the first two figures as Our Lady and St Joseph, seem to have had some difficulty in putting a name to the third figure. Thus Patrick Byrne:

> I saw the figures clearly, fully and distinctly, the Blessed Virgin, St Joseph and that of a bishop said to be St John the Evangelist.

Margaret Byrne (widow) said:

> I saw then and there distinctly the three images, one of the Blessed Virgin Mary, one of St Joseph and the third, as I learned, that of St John the Evangelist.

Bríd Ní Thrinsigh said:

> Agus an figiúir eile, a thógas mar Naomh Eoin, an Soiscéalaí, bhí sé ina sheasamh ar a clé. Chualas na daoine thart timpeall orm ag rá gurbh é íomhá Naoimh Eoin é.

> (And the other figure, which I took to be St John the Evangelist, was standing at her left. I heard those around me say that the image was St John.)

Earlier in her statement Bríd had said:

> Timpeall leath uair tar éis a seacht ar oíche 21ú Lúnasa, bhíos i dteach Bhean Uí Chathmhaoil, atá cóngarach don séipéal. Fad a bhíos ansin tháinig Máire Ní Bhroinn isteach agus dúirt sí go raibh radharc le feiceáil ag an séipéal nach bhfacamar riamh roimhe seo agus dúirt sí linn teacht agus é a fheiceail. D'fhiaf-

raíos di céard ab ea é agus duirt sí go raibh an Mhaighdean Bheannaithe, Naomh Iosaf agus Naomh Eoin le feiceáil ansin.

(About half past seven o'clock on the night of the 21st of August, I was in the house of Mrs Campbell which is quite near to the chapel. While I was there Mary Byrne came in and said there was a sight to be seen at the chapel such as we never before beheld and she told us to come and see it. I asked her what it was and she said that the Blessed Virgin, St Joseph and St John were to be seen there.)

Catherine Murray, aged eight and a half, said simply: 'I saw the Blessed Virgin Mary and St Joseph and St John or what was told me was the likeness of St John …'

Dominick Byrne, Senior, who was called 'to see the vision of the Blessed Virgin Mary and other saints at the south gable of the chapel' by his cousin and namesake Dominick Byrne, Junior, testified:

When I reached the south side of the chapel we saw the image of the Blessed Virgin Mary having her hands uplifted and her eyes turned up towards heaven, as if in prayer, and she was dressed in a white cloak. To her right I saw St Joseph and on her left St John, just as the other persons had told me before I came … The reason I had for calling the third figure St John is because some saw his statue or his likeness at Lecanvey parish chapel.

Margaret Byrne, sister of Mary and Dominick Junior, makes the same point in her evidence as Dominick Byrne, Senior, except that her recognition appears to be personal: 'The reason I knew St John was I saw a statue of him at Lecanvey chapel.' Dominick Byrne, Junior, notes in his deposition that he was called to the apparition by his sister. He reports:

I beheld the three likenesses or figures that have been already described, the Blessed Virgin, St Joseph and St John, as my sister called the bishop, who was like one preaching with his hand raised towards the shoulder and the forefinger and middle finger pointedly set, the other two fingers compressed by the thumb. In his left hand he held a book. He was so turned that he looked half towards the altar and half towards the people. The eyes of the images could be seen; they were like figures in as much as they did not speak.

Margaret Byrne, mother of Mary and of Margaret Byrne, testifies that she was called out to see the apparition by her daughter, Margaret. She continues:

It was raining when I came to the wall opposite the gable. I saw distinctly the three images or likenesses of the Blessed Virgin Mary, of St Joseph and, as I thought or heard, of St John the Evangelist ...

Mary Byrne, in her evidence to the 1879 commission, refers to the third figure in the apparition in the earlier part of her statement as,

the episcopal figure having the mitre on head, and the book of Gospels on his left hand.

At this stage of her evidence, she attaches no name to this third figure, although she specifically names the other two figures as Our Lady and St Joseph. Further along in her statement she says:

The third figure appeared to me to be that of St John the Evangelist. I do not know why I thought so, except the fact that at one time I saw a statue at the chapel of Lecanvey, near Westport, very like the figure I saw on the present occasion, holding the Gospel book and looking towards the altar.

She then adds:

I must remark that the statue I saw at Lecanvey chapel had no mitre on the head while the figure now beheld in the vision had one. The statue at Lecanvey had the book in the left hand and the fingers raised and it was this similarity of the figure and the pose that made me surmise that the third figure was the likeness of St John, the beloved disciple of Our Lord. I am not sure what saint particularly or especially this third figure symbolised. All I know is it appeared to me to be like that of St John the Evangelist.

Like her sister Margaret, Mary Byrne associates her identification of the third figure in the apparition with a statue in Lecanvey chapel which was of St John. In an account of the apparition given to a journalist (see Rynne p 19), she seems to suggest that it was owing to her identification that other people also identified the figure as St John. She states: 'I said, as I now expressed, that it was St John the Evangelist and then all the others present said the same – said what I stated.'

This ties in well with the references in the testimony of other witnesses to the fact that they learnt the identity of the third figure from others.

St John

Mary Byrne's testimony after she had identified the third figure as St John continues:

> The saint appeared to me to look to the altar which stood to the east side from him and towards the centre of the gable and under the window. The altar appeared to me to be a large full-sized altar, as is usually seen in Catholic churches. It had no candles or linens nor any ornamentation of a special kind, but above the altar and resting on it was a lamb with its face towards St John.

While Mary Byrne notes the fact that the saint was looking towards the altar and the lamb, she makes no further connection between St John and the altar and the lamb. This is true also of the testimony of several other witnesses who offer a simple description of St John, the altar and the lamb, but do not suggest any particular relationship between these three elements of the vision. Thus Patrick Hill details what he saw:

> An altar further on to the left of the statue or image of Our Blessed Lady and, above the altar, a lamb about the size of a newly weaned lamb, say a fortnight or three weeks old. Behind the lamb appeared the cross, lying, not elevated, and the body of the lamb a little removed in front of it and not resting on the wood of the cross. Around the lamb a number of gold-like stars

in the form of a nimbus or halo. This altar was placed right under the window outside, which is in the middle of the back of the church at Knock and more to the east of the figures.

Other witnesses who mention the altar and the lamb include Mary McLoughlin, housekeeper to Archdeacon Cavanagh, Parish Priest of Knock. She describes in one part of her evidence:

> An altar further on the left of the figure of the BVM and to the left of the bishop and, above the altar, a lamb about the size of that which is five weeks old. Behind the lamb appeared the cross. It was a bit away from the lamb, while the latter stood in front from it and not resting on the wood of the cross. Around the lamb a number of gold-like stars appeared in the form of a halo. (Rynne 45/46).

Among the visionaries who refer to the lamb and the altar, some say they did not see the cross, which is referred to by others. These symbols do not seem to have been understood with the same clarity nor described with the same precision as the human figures of Mary, Joseph and John. That part of the apparition which was more difficult to understand, and whose symbolism was perhaps not so clear to the visionaries, did not make the same immediate impression upon them as the more familiar figures of Mary, Joseph and the Beloved Disciple.

It is understandable that these more obscure elements of the vision did not make the same impact on the witnesses as the more familiar images from the first chapters of Matthew and Luke and from the beautiful verses of John 19, where Christ declares the disciple to be the true son of Mary and Mary to be the mother of every true disciple.

Yet we should note that the witnesses performed a singular service for us in identifying the linkage between St John and the vision of the altar and the lamb. It is up to us to see if we can, by any means, enter further into the meaning of this highly symbolic tableau.

Behold the Lamb of God (John 1)
In the first chapter of the Fourth Gospel, John the Baptist says of

Jesus: 'This was he of whom I said: He who comes after me, ranks ahead of me, because he was before me' (Jn 1:15), and again, 'among you stands one whom you do not know,the one who is coming after me; I am not worthy to untie the thong of his sandal' (Jn 1:26-27). But the most striking phrase John uses is, 'Here is the Lamb of God who takes away the sin of the world' (Jn 1:29).

And John's testimony continues:

> This is he of whom I said, 'After me comes a man who ranks ahead of me because he was before me. I myself did not know him; but I came baptising with water for this reason, that he might be revealed to Israel.' And John testified, 'I saw the Spirit descending from heaven like a dove, and it remained on him. I myself did not know him, but the one who sent me to baptise with water said to me, "He on whom you see the Spirit descend and remain is the one who baptises with the Holy Spirit." And I myself have seen and have testified that this is the Son of God' (Jn 1:30-34).

At this point in his gospel, John the Evangelist records a further incident where John the Baptist and two of his disciples encounter Jesus. John the Baptist points out Jesus saying: 'Look, here is the Lamb of God!' The two disciples heard him say this, and they followed Jesus. When Jesus turned and saw them following, he said to them, 'What are you looking for?' They said to him, 'Rabbi,' (which translated means Teacher) 'where are you staying?' He said to them, 'Come and see.' They came and saw where he was staying, and they remained with him that day. It was about four o'clock in the afternoon. One of the two who heard John speak and followed him was Andrew, Simon Peter's brother. He first found his brother Simon and said to him, 'We have found the Messiah' (which is translated Anointed). He brought Simon to Jesus, who looked at him and said, 'You are Simon son of John. You are to be called Ce'phas' (which is translated Peter). (cf. Jn 1:35-42).

The figure of the Lamb in St John's writings is a symbol heavy with meaning. It occurs more often in St John than in any other part of the New Testament.

A basic theme of John's message is the theme of the Word of God made flesh. Jesus is, indeed, a prophet greater than John; he is the 'Holy One of God', as St Peter says in John 6:69; but more than all these he is the true only-begotten Son of God, the Saviour of the World.

Mary Byrne makes the point in an interview (see Rynne p 147) that she felt that the preaching figure of St John in the apparition was preaching on the Lamb, 'something … like the last Gospel of the Mass.'

In the pre-Vatican II form of the Mass, there was a second or last gospel and it never changed. It was always Jn 1:1-14. Thus the visionaries of Knock would have been very familiar with the opening words of St John's Gospel, as they heard them every day at Mass:

> In the beginning was the Word, and the Word was with God, and the Word was God. … and the Word became flesh and lived among us, and we have seen his glory, the glory as of a Father's only son, full of grace and truth (Jn 1:1, 1:14).

Mary Byrne's intuition that John's preaching was on the incarnation, on the glory of Jesus in his passion and on the Lamb, points us towards a deeper understanding of the meaning of the apparition and its symbolism.

The writings which have come down to us under the name of St John, and which reflect the beliefs of John and of those who looked back to him as the Beloved Disciple and special confidant of Jesus, show that the theme of Jesus as the Lamb of God was a significant one for them. Among New Testament writings it is in those associated with John above all that we find the figure of the Lamb used and developed. The tradition which sees in Christ the Paschal Lamb, appears to go back to the very origins of Christianity. According to John, the death of Christ, and the very time it took place at the Pasch, would have been at the beginning of this tradition.

The Book of Revelation, the final book of the New Testament, also called the Apocalypse, describes the glory of Our Saviour who has died for our sins and is now entered into his glory.

In chapter five we read:

> The Lion of the tribe of Judah, the root of David, has conquered
> … and among the elders a Lamb standing as if it had been slaugh-
> tered … and the four living creatures and the twenty-four elders
> fell before the Lamb … They sing a new song … You are worthy
> to take the scroll and to open its seals, for you were slaughtered
> and by your blood you ransomed for God saints from every tribe
> and language and people and nation; you have made them to be a
> kingdom and priests serving our God and they will reign on earth
> … and I heard the voice of many angels … singing with full
> voice, Worthy is the Lamb who was slaughtered to receive power
> and wealth and wisdom and might and honour and glory and
> blessing. Then I heard every creature in heaven and on earth and
> under the earth and in the sea, and all that is in them, singing, To
> the one seated on the throne and to the Lamb be blessing and
> honour and glory and might forever and ever!

The Apocalypse contrasts strongly the weakness of the Lamb who
was sacrificed for our sins and the power which his heavenly exalt-
ation by the Father confers on Christ. The Lamb of God, Jesus, the
Word, is now entered into his glory, after his suffering. This is he
who is called faithful and true.

> He is clothed in a robe dipped in blood, and his name is called
> The Word of God. On his robe and on his thigh he has a name
> inscribed King of Kings and Lord of Lords (Rev 19:13, 16).

The theme of the Lamb, his suffering and his glory, occurs like a re-
frain in the Apocalypse. The Lamb is the Word of God. He is the
Saviour of the world. He is the same one who said:

> Very truly, I tell you, it was not Moses who gave you the bread
> from heaven, but it is my Father who gives you the true bread
> from heaven. For the bread of God is that which comes down
> from heaven and gives life to the world … I am the bread of life.
> Whoever comes to me will never be hungry, and whoever be-
> lieves in me shall never be thirsty' (Jn 6:32-35),

and again:

I am the living bread which came down from heaven. Whoever eats of this bread will live forever; and the bread that I will give for the life of the world is my flesh (Jn 6:51).

The Lamb in the Knock apparition, introduced by this figure of John, the Beloved Disciple, is the anchor point of the whole apparition. It is only because of Jesus' life, death and resurrection that Mary, his mother, can come to us in comfort and in silent appeal to prayer and to a life lived in accordance with his loving precepts. It is only because he has died and risen again that we can have hope of healing and the forgiveness of sins. It is only through his life and love, and to make it manifest to us, that she comes to visit us, to ask us, silently, to follow in his footsteps.

CHAPTER 3

Popular piety and Knock

Christopher O'Donnell, O.Carm.

*By the 1930s the gable had been restyled and statues of Our Lady,
St Joseph and St John, along with the altar, lamb and cross, had been
placed inside the railings.*

A feature of Knock pilgrimages from the beginning is both the local support from the people of Connacht, and the presence of pilgrims not only from other parts of Ireland, but from abroad. Those who come here find themselves at home and comfortable with what they find. We can come to a better understanding of Knock if we not only look to what is unique to it as a pilgrimage place associated with an apparition, but if we also place it within a wider context of religious practice. The religious practices of the people are often referred to as 'popular piety'. The word 'popular' here means 'of the people', to emphasise that these religious practices are spontaneous and come from the people themselves.

When we look at religious practice, we find a huge divergence. It covers pilgrimages, Latin fiestas, devotions, processions, prayers, folklore and many other manifestations. There is a real sense in which popular piety has a life and vitality independent of church authorities. Even if no bishop or priest were to advert to the last Sunday in July, thousands would still climb the Reek or Croagh Patrick. Again the practices on this holy mountain are traditional; they were not prescribed by a church authority and no one knows their origin. Similarly, we can say that, though diocesan and other pilgrimages are organised by church authorities, people also come to Knock quite independently of any encouragement received from hierarchy and clergy.

Popular Piety

It is only relatively recently that theologians and church teaching have devoted much attention to popular piety. It has always been around in the church from very early centuries. But reflection on its meaning is more recent. It is now seen as a way in which Christianity is incarnated in different cultures. In the late 1960s and early 1970s in Latin America, there was some withdrawal from, and criticism of, popular piety, particularly on the part of those who were involved in the struggle for justice. Social activists and liberation theologians saw this piety as an escape from commitment to the work for liberation, justice and peace. But, especially after an important meeting of the Latin American bishops at Puebla (1979), there was a revision of attitudes. Popular piety began to be seen as something deeply rooted in the culture and spirituality of peoples. The value of such piety was then recognised as having an important role in the emancipation of people and in the promotion of their culture.

Popular piety had earlier been studied at the 1974 Synod of Bishops. Its most important authoritative exposition was in the apostolic exhortation of Pope Paul VI on evangelisation (1976), *Evangelii nuntiandi* (article 48). The Pope is aware that popular piety can have error and superstition, but he is nonetheless convinced that it can be productive of great good. He goes on to say: 'It does indicate a certain thirst for God such as only those who are simple and poor in spirit can experience. It can arouse in people a capacity for self-dedication and the exercise of heroism when there is a question of professing the faith ... It can bear such excellent fruits and yet is fraught with danger.' The Pope sees popular piety as having 'an increasing contribution to make towards bringing the masses of our people into contact with God in Jesus Christ.'

Characteristics of popular piety

The first characteristic of popular piety is its roots in a people. It is not something that has been commanded by church authorities. The manifestations of such piety are very diverse: there are processions, prayers, wells, sacred images, actions, symbols and rites. There may also be liturgical celebrations, such as Mass or Benediction. The local bishop and clergy may well take part, especially if there are processions or liturgies. Popular piety is not systematic: it is not about one particular truth. Its meaning can only be grasped intuitively, and there may be different interpretations of the celebration. Popular piety is above all celebratory: it is frequently festive and spontaneous. However, at shrines there is often an element of penance and conversion.

Popular piety keeps in tension two vital truths. God and the saints are seen as far beyond us in their holiness; they are at the same time close and concerned with our needs. So in popular piety we find trusting and confident prayer.

When we look at Irish manifestations of popular piety we find above all a devotion to holy places. Whereas continental fiestas tend to fall on a particular day, Irish pilgrimages are to holy places such as wells, the churches of the saints and their burial places, throughout the year, with perhaps some special celebration on a particular day. The devotional exercises at a holy well or other sacred site are called 'stations'. In earlier centuries, there may have been psalms and perhaps a sermon or other instruction by a monk at the holy place. The carvings on the great high crosses depicted the story of salvation, especially the passion and glorification of Jesus. For simple people, the psalms were replaced by their own favourite prayers, especially the Our Father, Hail Mary, Glory be to the Father, Creed. These were usually said walking around the well or holy place. There was in some places a *rann* or special little prayer to the local saint. Most religions have the practice of walking around a holy place. It is perhaps noteworthy that invariably one walked in the direction of the sun, what the Irish call *deiseal*.

Popular piety and Mary

The two aspects of popular piety noted above are reflected in an important statement of Vatican II about the Virgin Mary: 'in holy Church she occupies the place which is highest after Christ and nearest to us' (Church Constitution 54). Though she is different from us in her sinlessness, in her supreme grace and holiness, we feel nonetheless that Mary understands our needs, our problems, our sin and failure.

There are thousands of shrines and popular celebrations in honour of the Virgin throughout the world. Whilst each one has its own characteristics, we can point to some features that are common to most Marian piety. Mary is patron of countries and cities; churches and boats are called after her; associations and societies take her name; in art she is represented as a member of all races, ethnic groups and peoples; she is dressed in the costumes of many civilisations. The message is that each people, each age, feels Mary to be one of their own. In many shrines we find a special emphasis on the Rosary. There are several reasons for this, not least the fact that the

Rosary is a prayer that is suitable for private recitation or for groups, and it does not involve organisation, clergy or a formal setting.

At the heart of popular piety associated with Mary is a profound sense that Mary, the sinless one, is the friend of sinners, that Mary in glory is the compassionate mother of the poor and the weak. Though Mary transcends us, she is never remote. These two themes are found in Knock from the beginning. All accounts of the apparition dwell on the poverty and distress of the people in the West of Ireland in 1879. Mary is seen as visiting her children in their need.

Popular piety and Knock

The modern station prayers at Knock were regularised in 1926 by the Archbishop of Tuam, Thomas Gilmartin, at the request of Father John Tuffy who was at Knock, 1919-1931.

The station at present comprises of several parts: first a visit to the Blessed Sacrament; the outdoor Way of the Cross; fifteen decades of the Rosary recited whilst walking around the old church; the Litany of the Blessed Virgin recited at the apparition gable of the old church; a second visit to the Blessed Sacrament during which the Creed is said, and prayers to Christ the King and to Our Lady of Knock are added. When there are large crowds or in inclement weather, these exercises are performed indoors, either in the old church or the new Basilica.

From the time of the apparitions, visits to the Blessed Sacrament, the Way of the Cross and the Rosary were very much a feature of Irish piety. They are the prayers of rural Ireland. It is not surprising that these are found from the beginning. When the outdoor Way of the Cross was erected in 1938, it was natural that it would feature in the station. There are records of the Litany of Our Lady being said or sung during the very first pilgrimages in 1880. The Rosary, said walking around the old church, is also very early. The first pilgrimage to Knock in 1880 processed around the church three times. It reflects the Irish practice at ancient holy places and wells.

In the very earliest pilgrimages, there was a blessing of water at Knock. There was, too, the custom of scraping the apparition wall and mixing the cement with this holy water which was then drunk. At a quite early stage the gable wall had to be protected from such practices and was several times resurfaced. People still bring blessed water home, thus extending into their ordinary lives the blessings they have prayed for at Knock. They use the blessed water for sick persons, for their animals and for various other needs. It is also a way in which those who cannot travel to Knock may feel associated with Mary's shrine.

Penance is an important feature of Knock from the beginning. It includes the Sacrament of Reconciliation, or confession. There has also been an emphasis on fasting. Walking barefoot to Knock and around the shrine was common at the beginning of this century. In earlier times, people also circled the church on their knees. Still very popular, and certainly penitential, are the all-night vigils which begin at midnight. A programme dating from 1936 shows that they comprised an hour of Eucharistic devotion, followed by an hour for private devotion, two hours for the full station, another hour for private devotion with a concluding Mass at 5 am. When Mgr Horan (+1986) was administrator, the format was slightly changed: Prayer service at midnight followed by a candlelight procession; a Eucharistic holy hour at 1.30; a half hour for private prayer, followed by the Way of the Cross at 3 am; the concluding Mass now at 4 am.

The same handbook – *Guidebook to Knock Shrine* which had its fourth edition in 1936 – is interesting in the hymns and devotions that it prints. The hymns include *Ave Maria, Sweet Sacrament Divine, Look Down O Mother Mary, O Mother I could Weep for Mirth, Nearer my God to Thee, Faith of Our Fathers* – as well as the common Benediction hymns in Latin. These hymns have that double tension that we noted as a characteristic of popular piety: they reach up to God and to Mary who are wholly other and yet are infinitely close.

One of the many hymns to Our Lady of Knock has the same twin focus:

> To welcome the balm of our sorrows,
> The Mother who watched thro' our woe …
> Our guiding star upwards and outwards,
> Whose blessed light hallows our soil
> Cead míle fáilte for ever
> To Mary, the Mother of God.
> (Hymn from 1880, author unknown)

Another processional hymn, set to music by Carl Hardebeck, has the same ideas:

> See she comes to Erin blessing,
> With her hands upraised in prayer,
> For us she has caressing
> For our sorrows she will bear.
> And the stars are sparkling round her,
> And the angels come and go,
> For Mary's love for Erin
> To her children she will show.

The Way of the Cross in this same booklet is in a tradition that is perhaps better known in the exercises of St Alphonsus Liguori. The reflections are an affective entering into the pain and sorrows of Jesus. At the same time, the Way of the Cross at Knock was penitential, with an act of contrition recited at each station and the Marian hymn, *Stabat Mater,* interspersed between the stations.

At that time, there was already a prayer to Christ the King. It will be noted that the feast of Christ the King had been established by Pius XI in 1925, that is, the year before the station prayers were organised with the approval of the Archbishop of Tuam. The prayer read:

> O Christ Jesus, I acknowledge Thee as universal King. All that has been made has been created for Thee. Exercise over me all Thy rights. I renew my baptismal promises by renouncing Satan, his pomps and works, and I promise to live as a good Christian. And especially I pledge myself to promote, according to my ability, the triumph of the rights of God and of Thy

Church. Divine Heart of Jesus, I offer Thee my poor actions to obtain the acknowledgement of Thy sacred Kingship by all hearts and thus the establishment of the reign of Thy peace in the entire universe. Amen.

At the time of the centenary of the apparition, this prayer was modified somewhat by Mgr Horan with the help of Tom Neary and others. Though the new version is more in keeping with modern piety, one might regret the dropping of the explicit renewal of baptismal commitment:

O Jesus, I honour you as my King and as King of the whole universe. All that I am and all that I have comes from you. Help me to be loyal and true to you always. Never let me betray you by the smallest sin. Give me the courage, at all times, to speak out in defence of you and of your church. May the peace of your Kingdom always reign in the hearts of men. O Jesus, I want you to be King of my heart and soul and all, and Mary to be my Queen. Amen.

The present station also has a prayer to Our Lady of Knock:

Our Lady of Knock, Queen of Ireland, you gave hope to your people in a time of distress and comforted them in sorrow. You have inspired countless pilgrims to pray with confidence to your divine Son, remembering his promise: 'Ask and you shall receive, seek and you shall find.' Help me to remember that we are all pilgrims on the road to heaven. Fill me with love and concern for my brothers and sisters in Christ, especially those who live with me. Comfort me when I am sick or lonely or depressed. Teach me how to take part ever more fervently in the Holy Mass. Pray for me now, and at the hour of my death. Amen.

This prayer has many elements: though addressed to Mary, it points to her Son; it invites confident supplication; it draws our attention to the need for practical charity; it recognises human needs, especially the loneliness and depression that so many people feel in the modern world.

A convergence of spiritualities

A most significant feature of Knock is the wide diversity of people who come there on pilgrimage. The thousands of letters sent each year to the shrine show some of the main reasons why people come to Knock and implore the intercession of the Virgin there. There are requests for crops, for sick animals, for children at school, for health, for relatives abroad, for family problems, for employment, and for those who have lapsed in faith. Thus all the needs of rural life are found, as well as the consequences of the pressures of modern urban society.

People come from many countries in the world, and from all social and ethnic groups. It is also notable that most Irish dioceses and many religious congregations have an annual pilgrimage day at the shrine. Other groups, like the international Eucharistic Legion and the Blessed Sacrament Guild, meet there. There are gatherings also of those with a very special focus, such as devotees of Padre Pio, those involved in Charismatic Renewal, members of the Legion of Mary.

All these associations, with their own spiritualities and special gifts in the church, can nevertheless find an environment in Knock in which they can be at ease. The traditional station, especially as modified today, shows that the shrine of Knock is not Marian in any narrow or exclusive way. The station prayers are at once traditional and timeless. Just as people going to holy places, like Clonmacnoise, saw the story of salvation unfolded in a high cross, so the modern pilgrim reflects with Mary on the passion of the Lord in the Stations of the Cross. The pilgrim then reflects, again with Mary, on the principal events in the life of the Lord as the fifteen decades of the Rosary are recited. The visit to the Blessed Sacrament, which begins the station, and the prayer at the apparition gable, where the sacrament is also reserved, are the Eucharistic context for the pilgrimage. The other prayers to Christ the King and to Our Lady of Knock, as well as the Creed, focus on the avoidance of sin, on faith, on practical virtue, and they recall Mary's intercession at the moment of death.

The station prayers cohere well with the apparition tableau. The joyful mysteries of the Rosary draw attention to the role of Mary and Joseph in the infancy of Jesus. The altar, the Lamb and the cross, as well as the figure of John, point to the sorrowful and glorious mysteries as well as to the events of the Way of the Cross. The Eucharistic visits, the Creed and the other prayers point to the need to incarnate the values of Knock in daily living. All the station exercises are integrated into the liturgies celebrated at the shrine.

The shrines of Lourdes and Knock have many things in common. Those who organised the shrine and its activities have clearly learned much from the great French shrine. The Marian emphasis is, however, different: in Lourdes the focus is on the Immaculate Conception, whereas in Knock it is on the Assumption. In both shrines the main focus is on Christ rather than on Mary; the centre of both shrines is Eucharistic. Lourdes and Knock both have the open meaning characteristic of popular piety. There is no one message or meaning, but the pilgrimage is experienced differently by each one who visits the shrine.

The popular piety found at Knock is a good illustration of the principles given by Pope Paul VI in his exhortation on the renewal of Marian devotion, *Marialis cultus* (1974).

The Pope asked that devotion take account of scripture, liturgy, ecumenism and anthropology, and he advocated the Rosary as a Marian devotion. The station is easily harmonised with scripture and liturgy; its Christocentricism and Eucharistic focus is surely helpful from an ecumenical perspective.

Finally, the anthropological has its place, for Knock has always seen the apparition as a visit of a gracious and loving mother to her children in their need. Knock, like every authentic Marian shrine, draws us to Christ and through him to the life of the Trinity. And the Irish tradition has long seen Mary as *Bean tí na Trionóide.*

CHAPTER 4

The meaning of pilgrimage

Michael Drumm

*In 1940 a flat-roofed oratory was erected at the apparition gable
and the statues, which had been in the open until then,
were enshrined inside.*

One of the most central characteristics of human behaviour throughout history has been the attraction to pilgrimage. Human beings are quite simply excited by travel and, if that be true of humans in general, that subset of humanity called the Irish seem to have an insatiable thirst for going on the journey. Now, of course it is true that not all journeys are pilgrimages, and that will become clear as we look at the nature of pilgrimage, yet the Irish have shown a particular propensity to travel. Maybe this helps to explain two of the most striking features of twentieth-century life on this island – the seemingly endless emigration throughout most of the century, and the startling numbers who volunteered as missionaries to go to very strange lands. Unquestionably there are more pertinent explanations for both of these phenomena, but I wonder have we ever reflected enough upon the nature of our itchy feet!

And itchy feet we surely have. It's hard to say for certain, as studies in this area are still in their infancy, but it is at least legitimate to claim that no country has been so influenced by pilgrimage as Ireland, and no people more formed by pilgrimage than Irish Catholics. These claims might seem extreme but there is a lot of evidence that one can adduce in their support.

Before looking at the history of pilgrimage, it's interesting to note that the actual study of pilgrimage is a very recent development. Why is it that, for centuries, all sorts of academics – historians, philosophers and theologians – basically ignored the very prevalent practice of pilgrimage? Maybe one of the reasons was embarassment, for undoubtedly one of the strangest aspects of religious behaviour is the activity of going on a pilgrimage. Why bother? What does one achieve? Is it a form of magic, believing that if one goes to a certain place and fulfills the ritual demands, then life will be changed for the better? And what on earth has it got to do with religious belief? We will see that interesting answers are beginning to emerge to these and similar questions.

What makes pilgrimage so interesting is not alone that many believers ignored it but that so many people, believers and non-believers alike, actually frowned upon the practice. Those who look at religious issues from a radically atheistic perspective probably see pilgrimage as the most pathetic form of religious enslavement, amounting to nothing more than witchcraft or superstition. It is then, I believe, necessary to explain the history and nature of religious pilgrimages if one is to facilitate a true understanding of our religious tradition by future generations, and if one is to issue the invitation to believers of the future to interpret and live ever anew our extraordinary religious heritage.

The story of pilgrimage in Ireland

From back in the mists of pre-history, it is now emerging that the people who lived on this island were always drawn to the holy place. These ancient holy places were primarily associated with large stones and wells. Why were our forebears so preoccupied with these stones and wells? One can easily understand the symbolism of the large stone – it is unchanging in a radically uncertain world, it appears to be everlasting when compared to the fragility of human life, and for people of the 'stone age' it was the very source of their power to manipulate their environment. The oldest remains of human life that have been discovered in Ireland are all stone structures, as if demonstrating just how durable they are. These remains date from the neolithic age (*lithos* is the Greek word for stone), meaning the new or later stone age, and are characterised most of all by megalithic (huge stone) tombs. So it is that differing examples of these megaliths (huge stones) are dotted all over the country, whether they be dolmens, passage graves or stone circles. Most of these were constructed between 3,500-2,500 BC. What's really interesting about them is that they have survived right down to today. How is it that they were not destroyed by the coming of the Celts or the Christians or the Normans; that they survived intact the cataclysm that was the Reformation in Ireland, and still stand even after the development of modern intensive agriculture? The wonders of the Boyne Valley in County Meath and Carrowmore in County Sligo, the two outstanding examples amongst the hundreds of megaliths in Ireland, bear eloquent testimony to our forebears on this island who sought permanence in the midst of life's transience, who touched something solid in the midst of everything ephemeral, and who spoke a word in silent stones five thousand years ago which we can still hear today.

In pre-historic times these great stones became centres of pilgrimage, holy places that people visited at special times. Although it is now impossible to reconstruct these pilgrimages, it is likely that people 'did the rounds', they walked around these mysterious stones whilst they prayed to their gods for a good harvest or fine weather or a safe passage through death to the other world. This tradition of doing the rounds of the holy place became a core element in Irish pilgrimage.

One should also mention other stones that are very significant in Irish tradition. The fascinating stone walls of the Céide Fields in County Mayo are a distant echo of the stone walls all over the west of the country. The wonderful stone constructions of the great Irish monasteries and friaries bear testimony to what might have been, but for the bloody suppression of the sixteenth century. One can still taste something of the mytery and magic of these stones in Aghaboe and Abbeyknockmoy, in Boyle and Ballintubber, in Clonmacnoise and Creevalea and in countless well-known and little-known stone ruins of churches and monasteries up and down the country. In the penal times that followed the suppression of these sanctuaries, Catholics buried their dead in the vicinity of these buildings for this was holy ground.

When the penal oppression was at its height, people gathered at other large stones for the celebration of the Eucharist; these Mass rocks themselves became places of pilgrimage for later generations who make the rounds of these rocks at appointed times of the year. So one can clearly see the significance of stones in the pilgrimage traditions of Irish Catholics, yet what is also very striking is that great cathedrals and basilicas have never become centres of pilgrimage for these same people. Think, for instance, of the old, beautiful, cathedrals of St Patrick and Christ Church in Dublin, and St Canice's in Kilkenny; I don't believe that Catholics visiting these jewels of our heritage have any sense of being pilgrims. Or think alternatively of the basilicas in Knock and on Lough Derg – these buildings, impressive as they are, especially in Knock, are not the key that unlocks the meaning of the pilgrimage. There's probably a message here as regards the true meaning of pilgrimage which we will return to later.

If stones are important in the history of Irish religious expression, then wells are just as significant. As the source of fresh water they were central in every culture that we know of. In Ireland, it appears that wells were holy places from the earliest times as people gathered to worship the gods of the earth, to pray for an abundant harvest and to celebrate merrily when the harvest came. The best way to analyse the tradition of making pilgrimages to holy wells is to start with the present practice in many parts of Ireland of still going to these wells at certain times of the year. These pilgrimages are sometimes called 'patterns' or 'patrons'. They are particularly popular in July and August, probably because these pilgrimages trace their roots to the Celtic festival of Lughnasa.

The old Lughnasa festival celebrated the first fruits of the harvest. Traditionally, this was the cutting of the first sheaf of corn. Later, with the emergence of the potato, it was the first digging of the new potatoes. The 'nasad' (games or assembly) of the god Lugh was a celebration of plenty, an offering of the first fruits of the harvest, the overcoming of hunger. The first fruits were there for all to see in the last days of July and the first days of August: there was new corn and new potatoes, the earth was yielding its fruit and there was much to celebrate. The fears of Bealtaine concerning the cow and dairy production, and of mid-summer's day with its fear of the crops failing to come to maturity, had passed. The hungry month of July, hungry because the remains of the previous year's harvest were probably already consumed, was over and the celebration could begin. People gathered on hills and at wells, they 'made the customary rounds, picked bilberries and wild flowers, danced, played and fell in love, raced and wrestled, competed in tests of strength and agility, joined in the routine fights, met old friends and exchanged news, heard old stories from the elders and grew to know the landmarks.'(M. MacNeill, *The Festival at Lughnasa*, p 66.)

They celebrated the land as they looked out over its mysterious beauty.

In the eighteenth and nineteenth centuries, the festival of Lughnasa, then known by a variety of names – Domhnach Chrom Dubh, Bilberry Sunday, Garland Sunday, etc. – was celebrated on the last Sunday of July (as it is to this day insofar as it is celebrated at all). It was still a festival of first fruits, not now the first sheaf of corn nor the slaughter of a lamb, but the first digging of the new potatoes. The new potatoes were dug at the end of July and the occasion was marked by ritual observance and boisterous celebration. Even in the homes of the poorest cottiers this was a special day, marked by a feast of mashed new potatoes with milk and seasoned with cabbage or onions known variously as *ceallaigh,* cally, colcannon, *brúightín,* bruisy or poundy. People went to the old Lughnasa sites to do the rounds and say their prayers. The festival commemorated and ensured the routing of the blight, the harvest was beginning and the first fruits were being celebrated. Maire MacNeill comments: 'It was the day when the sickle was first put to the ripened corn, as in later times it became the day when the spade turned up the first meal of potatoes. To that simple core much solemnity was added, and a great body of myth and ceremonial and popular custom accrued. Underneath it all, the consciousness remained of its essential character, perhaps nowhere so succinctly expressed as in the simple and ringing words of an old woman of the Ballinrobe district speaking of the day known locally as Domhnach Chrom Dubh, "The harvest is in and the hunger is over!"'(M. MacNeill, *The Festival at Lughnasa,* p 428.)

Catholicism did incorporate aspects of the feast into its rituals, while most of the features repugnant to Christian belief were suppressed – with the exception of faction fighting. Lugh was replaced by Patrick, the pilgrimages to holy wells continued, prayers were recited as one did the rounds of the stone or hill or well. Patrick had the same powers as Lugh – to protect the crops, to lend importance to a certain place, to overcome the forces of evil. The gatherings in each place developed a link with a particular saint and became known as 'patterns' or 'patrons'. So it is that even today the residue of the ancient festival of Lughnasa is present in the pilgrimage practice of Irish Catholics.

A particularly good example is the pilgrimage to 'Tobar nAlt' on the shores of Lough Gill near Sligo. Of old, this was a Lughnasa gathering in late July or early August, where people gathered at the holy well to celebrate the first fruits of the harvest. In penal times, Mass was offered on a large rock beside the well, and today, on the last Sunday of July, known locally as Garland Sunday, pilgrims gather for Mass and do the rounds by following the Stations of the Cross.

It is interesting to note the development of such a pilgrimage centre over centuries, since it is like a shaft driven into history, uncovering several successive layers of religious consciousness. Of old, it would have been a place of merriment, dance, music and games as the folk celebrated the first fruits of a new harvest; in the post-Reformation penal times it was a symbol of defiance, and since the famine of the 1840s it has become a penitential pilgrimage where people seek to atone for personal sin. So one can see the shift from the raucous religious expression of an earlier age to the personal scrupulosity and private piety so characterisitic of post-famine Irish Catholicism. Nowhere is the change more striking than in music and song: at the traditional Lughnasa gatherings there would have been gaiety and dance and music in the air, whilst the post-famine hymns were doleful and sad; we moved as a people from a celebration of life and merriment to a preoccupation with sin and sorrow. The renaissance in traditional Irish music suggests a re-awakening of a dormant spirit, a lively spirit that would lift the hearts of the pilgrims.

Yet underneath our more recent expressions one still finds the vestiges of the pilgrimage practices of an earlier time. In the festival of the Galway Races in late July, and the public holiday on the first Monday of August, one finds the residue of the Lughnasa festival. Isn't it interesting that the only two countries with public holidays in early August are the Republic of Ireland and Scotland? Yet the idea of celebrating the first fruits of the harvest, or indeed the completion of the harvest in early autumn, has long since evaporated from Irish Catholic consciousness; in fact, in an extraordinary irony, it is looked upon as a Protestant celebration. This is indeed ironic as Irish Catholics traditionally celebrated the mysterious sacredness of the earth, and what could be more mysterious or wondrous than the new harvest?

Pilgrimage always involves a certain hardship, but it also needs to be a celebration of the wonder of life. Such a celebration must engage all the senses, not just sight and sound but, even more importantly, taste, touch and smell. Irish Catholics have always gone on pilgrimage in order to touch the source of blessing and healing. Such a sense of touch is at the heart of what it means to be an Irish Catholic; one touches the Mass rock or the stone or the statue or the well since touch and taste are the most evocative of the senses. And this sense of touch has other expressions: in the distribution of ashes on Ash Wednesday and the kissing of the cross on Good Friday, we touch the mystery of suffering; in the newly ordained priest we touch the hands of blessing; in the corpse of a loved one, or even just the coffin of an unknown stranger, we touch the mystery of death. This idea of touching the sacred is at the very heart of Irish pilgrimage tradition – at the goal of the pilgrims' journey one can touch some power that one cannot touch at home. That is the very reason for going on a pilgrimage.

The story of Christian pilgrimage

Pilgrimage, not least in Ireland, long pre-dates the emergence of Christian belief. But Christianity developed new forms of pilgrimage to celebrate its own emerging identity. The earliest Christians adopted the Jewish idea of being the pilgrim people of God awaiting the return of the Lord; they cried 'maranatha' – 'come Lord Jesus' and bring our earthly pilgrimage to an end. But when the end did not come as soon as expected, and Christianity spread all over the Roman Empire, attitudes began to change.

The key change occurred in 312 when the Emperor Constantine issued an edict tolerating Christianity. This was in stark contrast with even the recent history of Christians in the Roman Empire, for as late as the early 300s AD they had suffered a terrible persecution under the Emperor Diocletian. The blood of martyrdom was one of the great sources of Christian inspiration and, with their new found freedom, Christians turned the tombs of martyrs into great pilgrimage centres.

The most important martyrs had been slain in Rome, since Christian tradition held that Peter and Paul were martyred in the city probably during the persecution of Nero in the mid-60s AD. Now that they had the freedom to build, Christians adopted the Roman basilica to their own needs and erected large monuments over the tombs of Peter and Paul. Christian Rome would henceforth become a centre of pilgrimage for Christians throughout the world.

But if Rome was important, then Palestine, the holy land, was to become equally important. A key figure in the development of Christian pilgrimage to Palestine was Helena, the mother of the Emperor Constantine. She visited Jerusalem and discovered what was believed to be the true cross; a huge basilica called the Holy Sepulchre was erected on the site. This too became a centre of pilgrimage.

Thus it was that Rome and Palestine became centres of pilgrimage for Christians. As one journeyed on one's earthly pilgrimage, it became a great source of inspiration to touch the heart of one's faith by making a pilgrimage to these holy places. And touch was all important – the pilgrim didn't make this extraordinary journey just to look at things but rather to feel and touch and taste the very origins of their belief. This is probably the reason for the emergence of the overwhelming interest in relics. Early on, the church believed that the remains or relics of the great saints – Peter, Paul, the other apostles and individuals like Martin of Tours around whom an amazing cult developed – should be left undisturbed. But as the church developed, this tradition changed for various reasons: the barbarian invasions of the city of Rome in the fifth century necessitated the removal of remains from tombs in order to protect them; the Islamic invasion and takeover of Palestine initially put a stop to Christian pilgrimage to the holy land and sowed the idea in the minds of political and religious leaders of transporting the relics, particularly of apostles, from Palestine to major centres in Europe which were not closed to Christians. This latter trend was open to terrible abuse as metropolitan centres vied with each other for the fame and economic benefits associated with becoming a shrine of apostolic significance. Rome remained the most important centre with its four great basilicas: St Peter's with the tomb of Peter, St Paul's with the tomb of Paul, the Lateran Cathedral with relics of Peter and Paul, and St Mary Major's with the relics of Christ's birth from Bethlehem.

But Rome did not become famous and popular as a pilgrimage centre *because of* the dominance of Moslems in Palestine. However this was indeed the case with the town called Compostela in Galicia in Northern Spain.

Santiago de Compostela became the most popular pilgrimage centre in Europe in the eleventh and twelfth centuries. Many Christians were finding it difficult to travel to Palestine and, in the religious fervour that was unleashed around the time of the millennium, their attention was turned westwards to a Celtic region of Northern Spain where there was a strong legend that James the Apostle, the son of Zebedee and the brother of John, had visited Spain during his lifetime, was the first of the apostles to have been martyred in Jerusalem and that his body had been mysteriously transported to Compostela after his death. Here then was the tomb of not just a martyr but a martyr who was an apostle. In the heady days of the new millennium, pilgrimage laid hold of the European imagination; the end of the world had not come, as many had feared, but it surely could not be far off and one needed to prepare the way through penitential pilgrimage. The most famous penitential pilgrimage was to Santiago (St James) de Compostela, far off in the Celtic mists of Northern Spain. A pilgrims' path was constructed all the way from Northern France, whilst the monks of Cluny challenged and encouraged the pilgrims. Churches in the romanesque style were built all over the south-west of France and the north of Spain, almost as staging posts on the way to Compostela. The new millennium had begun with intense religious fervour.

Another interesting example of a popular pilgrimage in medieval Europe was the shrine of St Thomas à Becket in Canterbury. Thomas was murdered in Canterbury Cathedral on 29 December 1170, and almost instantly his tomb became a focus for pilgrimage. Throughout the high middle ages, as recounted in Chaucer's *Canterbury Tales,* all sorts of folk came for all sorts of reasons to the tomb of St Thomas of Canterbury.

There is no doubt whatsoever but that abuses developed around many of these pilgrimage centres. The most theologically significant was the widely held perception that one could almost purchase salvation by enduring a pilgrimage of sufficient severity. This was why Martin Luther and the Protestant Reformation in general made such a strident attack on all forms of pilgrimage. Henry VIII put an end to any further pilgrims' tales about Canterbury, and centres like Santiago de Compostela went into decline, but in the Celtic mists of another land on the periphery of Europe, Henry VIII's Reformation tried in vain to put a halt to pilgrimage. The story of Christian pilgrimage in Ireland was so deeply rooted that the Reformation failed to destroy it.

Christian pilgrimage in Ireland

We now need to bring together the two themes that we've been analysing – the story of Irish pilgrimage and the story of Christian pilgrimage. Christian pilgrimage in Ireland evolved differently from elsewhere, for many reasons. Probably the most important reason was the absence of martyrdom in the coming of Christianity to these shores. Today it is impossible to reconstruct the interaction of early Christianity in Ireland with the pre-existing Celtic religious traditions, but one thing seems fairly obvious and that is that it wasn't a bloody encounter. Christian belief and Celtic traditions became so intertwined that it was only in the cataclysm of the Reformation that we meet the first Irish martyrs.

Among the earlier saints, Patrick and Brigid were characterised as heroic figures like the Celtic gods before them, and of the others, Colmcille, Columbanus, Fergal, Brendan, Kilian, Fiacre and Gall must surely be cast in the ranks of the greatest adventurous travellers in history. These were no tourists but rather those who embraced *peregrinatio pro Christo,* pilgrimage for Christ. The difference in this type of pilgrimage was, of course, that it lasted for life as these pilgrims set out on a journey from which they would never return. The enormous effect of their efforts on the subsequent history of Europe surely demonstrates how efficacious the life of the pilgrim can be. Even in distant places like Salzburg in Austria, St Gallen in Switzerland, Bobbio in Italy, Würzburg in Germany and hundreds of other towns and cities, the stories of these pilgrims are still recounted. But the free wandering spirit of these Irish pilgrims for Christ led to difficulties with political/religious authorities who wanted a more settled form of church life; as ever, the 'itchy feet' were causing the Irish some difficulty.

Like people from other lands, Irish folk went to Jerusalem, Rome and Compostela throughout the middle ages, but there were also pilgrims who came to our shores from Europe. St Patrick's Purgatory on Lough Derg held great fascination for the European pilgrims who visited it in medieval times. In travelling across the harsh land and seas to the frontiers of the known world, Lough Derg became for foreign visitors almost like a journey to the other world where they encountered suffering and death. The native Irish, as ever, had a different perception of things: Lough Derg was not so much an encounter with the next world as with the reality of this world. It was and remains a harsh penitential pilgrimage, but it can only be properly understood in the context of the overall pattern of pilgrimage in Ireland including holy wells, mountains, great stones and islands. Some of these pilgrimages were extremely severe whilst others were joyous, boisterous celebrations. In one manner or another, many aspects of these pilgrimages are still prevalent. In order to understand why this is the case, we need to look briefly at the meaning of pilgrimage.

The meaning of pilgrimage

Given all that we have said so far, the fundamental question surely is not what is pilgrimage, or when does it take place, but why, why over centuries have Irish people been drawn to pilgrimage? There are many possible answers to this question. I will comment upon just one. To go on pilgrimage is to separate oneself from the ordinary; the very act of travelling away from home is a separation; the more difficult the journey, the more one becomes aware that something different is beginning. This is why some pilgrimages demand that the pilgrims walk or fast or go barefoot. These rituals facilitate a different form of interaction between the pilgrims; pilgrims tend to talk and listen to each other in a different way than if they met in the shop or the pub or at home. Since pilgrimage centres tend to be at the periphery of things, people must leave their homes to go up the mountain, over to the island, visit the ruin, do the rounds of the old graveyard or Mass rock or holy well. This very peripherality is important because life looks different from the edge; one gets a different angle on ordinary things from the mountain top or the island or the well. Of course you can go to these places on your own, but true pilgrimage tends to create a new community with one's fellow pilgrims, even though they might be complete strangers. Isn't it interesting that, in ordinary life, especially today in the city where most people now live, one does not talk to strangers, yet this is precisely what happens on pilgrimage?

At the goal of true pilgrimage our sense of fellowship is strengthened, our perception of things is broadened, our awareness of mystery is deepened, our identity is renewed, our wounds can be healed. And then one goes home, back to the ordinary routine which is often tedious and boring, but one knows that there is more to life than meets the eye for, at some point in the future, one can return to that mountain or ruin or stone or well, and every time one does so it is as if one enters into communion with the strangers who are long since dead and the strangers one meets on the road. One can indeed make a pilgrimage completely on one's own, but if it is truly a pilgrimage it will awaken one to communion with the earth, with the dead, with the lonely, with those living in need of healing, for the ultimate insight of the pilgrim is that there are no strangers, only fellow pilgrims.

But surely pilgrimage is now coming to an end? It was understandable in older days but we've now grown into a new religious and psychological maturity. Everyone knows, as Protestants have always pointed out, that one does not need to go on pilgrimage to be saved and they are absolutely right; anyone who suggests otherwise is simply wrong. So should we not stay at home, put our trust in God and try to live Christian lives? The answer is 'yes' for those who want to, but many others in the course of their pilgrimage from birth to death, from the womb to the tomb, from our mysterious origin to our mysterious destiny, will want to touch this mystery in a particular place at a particular time. And so they will go on pilgrimages to the shrines and places that lift their spirits, that heal their wearied souls, that nourish them for life's journey. Putting a stop to pilgrimages in Ireland, which many political and religious leaders have attempted over the ages, is impossible. Rather than criticising it, we should attempt to harness this remarkable tradition for the future. The story of pilgrimage amongst the people of this island is a crucial part of who we are. Pilgrimage has had a long past in this land, but it can also have a future.

The future of pilgrimage

Briefly, I would like to identify four key perspectives relevant to the future of pilgrimage in Ireland.

(1) The turn of the last millennium witnessed a huge upsurge in pilgrimage throughout Christian Europe. As we enter the new millennium travel is still popular – tourism is the fastest growing industry in the world. When tourists today visit significant archaeological sites, art galleries and museums, their responses are something akin to pilgrims of old: they are often full of awe and wonder, they see things differently from before, and sometimes their hearts are truly uplifted. But, of course, a tourist is not a pilgrim, yet surely a tourist is a potential pilgrim, especially in an age of renewed interest in spirituality and mysticism. However, the problem is that this interest in things spiritual and religious is very private and individualistic; what we need to harness most of all is a new sense of communal identity. Pilgrimage can help us in this because creating unexpected bonds among strangers has always been one of its strengths.

(2) This is the era of privatisation. Whatever the merits of privatisation in the world of politics and economics, it's a pretty fatal force in the world of religious belief. If our lives are predicated only on the value of efficiency then we will miss out on much that is of true value. That is why all religious traditions emphasise the importance of a sabbath where, quite literally, we take time off so that we can become more human. To work all the time, to rush and run so much that one almost forgets that one is alive, is inhuman. Pilgrimage is a great antidote to market forces – it is completely inefficient and, by any economic standards, a total waste of time. Some of the words that came into our language from pilgrimage traditions give us a hint of the spirit of the pilgrim: to canter is to follow in the steps of those who went to Canterbury, to roam is to behave like pilgrims to Rome, to saunter (*Sant Terre* – Holy Land) is what one should do in a holy place like Palestine. Pilgrims should not be in a hurry, otherwise they become only tourists.

(3) There is today a renewed interest in all things Celtic – music, art, folklore and spirituality. One of the most crucial dimensions of Celtic spirituality, as we saw earlier, was pilgrimage. Many of the Celtic pilgrimage traditions died away in the aftermath of the famine of the 1840s, and the pilgrimages which survived that unspeakable horror tended to become overlaid with guilt, the demand for temperance in all things, and personal sorrow. We now know that there was a whole other dimension in Irish pilgrimage tradition that was more joyful and celebratory. Maybe we need to bring these two strands together in the pilgrimage practice of the next millennium.

(4) Knock is now the greatest Irish pilgrimage centre. It is unique in that it is both part of the modern European Catholic tradition of Marian apparitions and clearly part of the long Irish tradition of pilgrimage. In order to appreciate what its future might be, one must understand the context in which pilgrimage to Knock began. Hunger stalked the land of Ireland many times in the nineteenth century; most shockingly of all, it revisited the people of Connacht thirty years after the Great Hunger, in the late 1870s. In 1879 the poor of North Connacht were in a wretched state. There was noth-

ing to celebrate around Lughnasa time as the potato crop failed for
the third year in a row, and on 21 August several people claimed to
see a Marian apparition on the gable wall of the church in Knock.
Michael Davitt's land war was about to begin and the word 'boy-
cott' would soon enter the English language. Pilgrimage to a shrine
like Knock must never become a way of escaping the problems of
the world, but in the great tradition of Irish pilgrimage it should
awaken in pilgrims a renewed sense of communion with those
strangers who are hungry, oppressed, downtrodden and rejected.

(5) All of the earth is holy ground, but from the earliest biblical
times there have been special places to remind us of this truth.
Never were we more in need of true sanctuaries – holy places to
which we can withdraw for reflection and renewal. Such sanctuaries will be different for different people – some will withdraw to the
quiet of their own room, some will visit a peaceful church, but at
times we all need to go on pilgrimage to a great shrine like Knock
or a mountain or a well or a rock or a ruin. Even if you go to such a
sanctuary completely on your own, the spirit of the true pilgrim
will be awakened to the beauty of the earth, the struggle of life, the
wonder of who we are, the heartbreak of letting go, and the short-
ness of our lives. And, of course, the pilgrim grows in awareness
that on life's journey there are no strangers, only fellow pilgrims.
There is no more important message for humanity as the third millennium dawns.

CHAPTER 5

Healing and Reconciliation

Angela Forde and Donal Flanagan

*The 1940 oratory was replaced by this glass and steel structure
in time for the Papal Visit in 1979.*

PART I: HEALING

Angela Forde

To write about Knock brings a kaleidoscope of images before my eyes: not just the crowds on a busy pilgrimage Sunday nor the candlelight procession after the evening session of the Novena, nor wheelchairs being wheeled into the Basilica, but also a young couple hand in hand on the grounds; denim clad youngsters touching the panel of stone from the apparition gable; a business man parking his car, pocketing his mobile phone and making his way to the shrine; people quietly praying in the Apparition Chapel; tourists wandering around clutching their camcorders; a Down's syndrome adult accompanied by aged parents; grandmother, daughter and grandchildren on a three-generational visit to Knock; pilgrims sitting quietly looking at the flowers on a fine summer's day, and the trickle of people into the Confessional Chapel in mid-winter.

Each one who comes has a personal story and each story is so different. There is the young man awaiting the results of a HIV test who tells his family he is going to a Rock Festival and spends the weekend in Knock instead. There is the old woman who has carried the story of sexual abuse in silence for seventy years and needs to tell somebody before it is too late. There are parents grief-stricken because of the death of a child. There is the loneliness of a mother coming to terms with the news of terminal cancer. No matter what the story, all are on pilgrimage.

Some have consciously set out on a pilgrim journey, others find themselves drawn here without quite knowing why, and others, ambivalent about coming, use the excuse of bringing somebody else. And I hear 'Knock is special.' 'I don't know why I am here.

Something drew me in.' 'I've got so much from Knock.' 'There is a great peace here.' 'I thought I'd just come and say a few prayers.' 'I had no place else to go.' A need, conscious or unconscious, draws them to Our Lady's Shrine and it is often a need for healing, wholeness and reconciliation.

As soon as the news of the apparition spread, people began to come to Knock. Today 1.5 million people visit the shrine in the course of a year. From the beginning, pilgrims came seeking physical healing for themselves and for loved ones, or to pray for deliverance from some hurt or pain or emotional wound. It was inevitable that this would happen. Pain and suffering are always among the greatest problems encountered in life. In the face of suffering and difficulties we experience our powerlessness, our limitations and our finiteness. Suffering surfaces the big questions – Who is God? What is the meaning of life? Why me? In the face of human limitations, we are drawn to the infinite, to the transcendent, to what is greater than ourselves, and particularly to those places where it seems the veil between this world and the Beyond has been lifted for even a brief time.

Many who visit places of pilgrimage have stories of healings of one kind or another, and Knock is no exception. Things happen which do not seem to happen so readily in other places. Is there an explanation for this? Coming on pilgrimage involves a physical journey, a physical journey which of its very nature puts the traveller in touch with the other two great journeys of life – the journey inwards towards the heart of who I am, and the journey towards God. Coming to a place of pilgrimage creates a space, a time for reflection and allows what is most deeply human, the capacity for self-reflection. As one sets out on a pilgrim journey, human problems and difficulties come to the surface and matters which were pushed to the background or repressed begin to demand attention. Coming to Knock and stepping into the shrine grounds is leaving the ordinary circumstances of life and stepping into a place where faith is foremost. It is the crossing of a threshold, the entrance to a space where countless thousands have prayed for more than a hundred years. This is holy ground. There are Masses, Rosaries, processions, hymns and prayers. Everything else falls into the background, and God and his power to heal, through the intercession of Our Lady of Knock, comes into sharp focus.

God's healing power is everywhere, but in a sacred place people are more receptive and so the power of God's healing can begin to work for them. Sometimes the healings that take place on pilgrimage are very direct and miraculous, the blind see, the deaf hear, the dumb speak and the lame walk. But more often the healing is an inner healing which is begun in a much less spectacular manner. Many come to Knock praying for a miracle and hoping for a direct intervention from on high. The reality is that God does not do directly for us what we can do for ourselves. God wants us to use the human means at our disposal and in that way be healed.

When we talk of healing and reconciliation, it is important that these have a threefold aspect. As human beings we are body, mind and spirit. These are three dimensions of the one reality, and all are interconnected. There is not a physical life as distinct and separate from the emotional life. There cannot be an emotional life which is not embodied, nor a spiritual life over and above the other two. Healing is about wholeness, and to be healed as human beings the healing must be integrated into the threefold aspects of our life. Reconciliation is about reconciliation with God, with our neighbour and with ourselves, and again these three areas are inextricably linked. It is a bit like the mystery of the Trinity, 'Three in One and One in Three.'

However, individual pilgrims do come with a need in one particular area in sharper focus than in another. Knock as a place of healing and reconciliation provides nourishment for body, mind and spirit, and opportunities to explore at least the different aspects of reconciliation. The human means are provided with a hope and trust that God's power to heal and save will be at work.

If we think of healing and reconciliation in this way, the very first aid provided in Knock is the space and beauty of the grounds. To have a place to sit quietly with one's thoughts can begin the healing process. Trees, flowers, birdsong delight the senses and lift the spirit, as do the muted colours of stained glass and the sound of organ music. For the Prodigal Son (Lk 15), the act of coming to his senses was the first step on his journey back to his father's house. So it can be for the person broken and hurt by life's experiences.

Then there are the sacramentals – holy water, the blessing of the sick, the blessing of religious objects, a guided prayer session, the lighting of candles – all of which put the pilgrim in touch with the sacred and open him/her up to co-operate with God's healing power.

Many who come are not even aware that healing begins at such a level, or how such things work on them, but they are aware of other aspects of Knock which appear more specifically geared towards healing. Every day during the pilgrimage season, hundreds of people receive the Sacrament of the Sick, that sacrament which is especially intended for those who suffer from sickness and infirmity. In Knock it is celebrated in the context of the Eucharist and all present are invited to surround the sick with their prayers and concern. The priest prays, 'Through this holy anointing may the Lord, in his love and mercy, help you with the grace of the Holy Spirit. May the Lord who frees you from sin save you and raise you up.' To be present at the anointing in a full Basilica of praying people is often to have an almost tangible sense of God's touch rendering peace. The number who are raised up in a physical manner is very small, but many report feeling raised up and strengthened at an emotional and spiritual level.

The other great sacrament of healing, the Sacrament of Reconciliation is also easily available. Every day of the year except Christmas Day and St Stephen's Day, confessions are heard for a minimum of seven hours. Knock is unique among the Marian Shrines of the world for the number of people coming to confession. It is also unique in having a purpose built Chapel of Reconciliation. The sacrament has always been part of the traditional Knock devotions and, as the numbers coming to Knock have increased, so have the numbers celebrating the sacrament of God's forgiveness – as many as six thousand per week in the pilgrimage season. The new Chapel of Reconciliation, where sixty priests can hear confession at any one time, gives pilgrims a place of quiet reflection and prayer to prepare for, and make thanksgiving in the presence of, the Blessed Sacrament. There is ample opportunity to be reconciled, to be freed to seek reconciliation with others, and to be imbued with the hope of making a new future possible.

While many find solace and healing in the sacrament, the confessors over the years became increasingly aware that individual penitents needed more time and more expertise than they could provide in the confessional. Some of the problems they met were not necessarily of a confessional nature but needed attention if the pilgrim was to be able really to acknowledge and experience God's forgiveness and healing. Since the care of the pilgrim as a whole person is at the heart of what Knock is about, from this expressed need grew the idea of providing a Counselling Service. When the Chapel of Reconciliation was built, a counselling area was included and a part-time service provided on busy pilgrimage days. The demand for the service was such that it confirmed the need for a full-time service and that is now in place.

The Counselling Service in Knock is a professional service and, in that, it is no different from any other counselling service. It provides people with an opportunity to explore their experiences, particularly in relation to the problems of living. Counselling is characterised by listening, acceptance and confidentiality. The service is not confined to pilgrims or those going to confessions but is open to everybody, including people who have no church or faith affiliation. Like with any other counselling service, people present with varied problems – difficulties in relationships, those who are grieving, those who have been physically or sexually abused, those coping with illness – their own or others, those with low self-esteem and a sense of failure. People also come who have 'growth' issues, a sense that there is more to life than what presents at a particular time. And many come who feel there is something they need to talk about and would like to explore it in a gentle, non-threatening way. The Counselling Service provides the opportunity to work on these matters in an on-going counselling relationship.

Many ask why there is need for counselling now, and particularly in Knock. We live in a very different age than did the visionaries. A visit to the Folk Museum, with even a cursory glance at the photographs and artefacts, speaks of a different Ireland. 1879 was a year of famine, hunger, poverty, and emigration stalked the land. The increased prosperity of recent years has done much to eliminate these scourges, but the emotional damage caused by hardship, emigration and isolation continues to affect the lives of many individuals and families in the West of Ireland. That pain runs deep in the Irish psyche and the psychological scars are far from healed. The killer diseases then were the infectious diseases (TB, diphtheria, typhoid and the like.) Medical science has dealt effectively with these. Every age, however, has its own malaise and, in the modern age, it more often has its origin in the mind or the spirit than in the body. The modern world has become increasingly complex. Many people experience confusion and inadequacy. There is a huge sense of fragmentation and uncertainty. Trying to keep pace with the rate of change often leads to confusion and stress. Institutions of church and state, which in former times provided answers, no longer seem able to do so. Old taboos are lifted. There is less support from the extended family. The stress and strain of all of this begins to show at a physical, emotional or spiritual level.

Counselling is one way to deal with some of this. As increased prosperity eliminates physical hunger and the struggle to survive is no longer centre stage, other hungers surface and other needs emerge. There is a need for space and opportunity to get in touch with deeper questions. Issues of meaning surface – Who am I? Where am I going? How can I be more truly who I am? Teilhard de Chardin pointed out in his writings that human evolution in our day is at the level of consciousness, and those questions are part of that evolution. Counselling can be a forum to explore those issues and can lead to a greater sense of integration, healing and wholeness.

What is unique about a Counselling Service in Knock and how does it fit in with the nature of pilgrimage? Coming on pilgrimage brings the need for healing, at whatever level, to the fore and there is often a willingness and an openness to face the inner journey. The drop-in nature of the service at busy times means that there is often a match between the moment of readiness and the availability of a skilled listener. As one American pilgrim put it, 'It is awesome that this can happen'. One meeting with a counsellor is obviously not adequate to deal with an issue but it can help to validate the pilgrim's experience, give a taste of what counselling is about, and provide a referral to a counsellor nearer home. It can also help to give some sense of what the philosopher Martin Buber meant when he wrote that 'the healing is in the meeting.'

It is not without reason that the service is situated in the Chapel of Reconciliation. For some, the Counselling Service can be a kind of transitional space on the way to celebrate the sacrament. Aspects of forgiving self and others can be dealt with before celebrating God's forgiveness. Like the Prodigal Son the pilgrim can then 'leave this place and go to the Father'. Take, for instance, the pilgrim who had not been to confession for over thirty years, who had forgotten how to go but was filled with such a yearning to be part of a church community that she would sneak into the back seat at non-Catholic services (feeling she was not even worthy to enter a Catholic church). On a very short visit to Knock, the Counselling Service provided her with an opportunity to explore her fears and guilt, to prepare to ask for the sacrament, and to be personally introduced to a priest. It also means that those who have received the sacrament, and still do not feel at peace with themselves or others, can explore the problem in more depth. Emotional healing takes time. They can be helped to understand that what is framed as a spiritual problem has a human dimension, and that it is only as the human issues are unravelled that we can be truly open to the spiritual. 'I cannot pray contemplatively any more' has very little to do with prayer, but much to do with the ungrieved loss of a loved one.

The pilgrim comes

> 'a smile on her face
> Though her mind may be bleeding from old
> And new wounds …
> And in the silence a story is told.'
> (*The Pilgrim*, Brendan Kennelly)

There are different ways of telling the story. Some tell it in silence to their God, others tell it to themselves, owning it for the first time. Others speak it aloud in confession, in the counselling room, or to a stranger on the grounds. The place, the prayer, the overall atmosphere in Knock creates an environment which supports the pilgrim in facing and naming his/her story. In Patrick Kavanagh's poem, 'Having Confessed', there is the line: 'God cannot catch us unless we stay in the unconscious room of our heart.' There is much at Our Lady's Shrine that brings one into that place, so that God's healing power can touch many a pilgrim.

To face oneself and to face one's God is a transformative experience. The pilgrim leaving Knock is like the disciple coming down from the mountain of Transfiguration and facing once more into the or- dinary and the everyday; all may seem the same, yet something has changed. For some, a visit to Knock is the end of a journey towards healing and reconciliation; for others, it is the beginning of that journey; and for all it is part of the journey towards God which happens 'in the bits and pieces of everyday' (*The Great Hunger,* Patrick Kavanagh).

PART II: RECONCILIATION

Donal Flanagan

The Chapel of Reconciliation was dedicated on 15 July, 1990. It is a low unobtrusive building, almost concealed from view. A quiet place, a place for reflection and prayer, a place focussed on the interior life and on the Sacrament of Reconciliation. Above the highest point of the building rises a cross, the sign of God's love and of his mercy. There could be no simpler or clearer statement of the purpose of the building – to be the place where God offers us divine reconciliation and peace through the ministry of priests in sacramental confession.

Approaching the chapel, one has the sense of entering a place of shelter, a place of refuge, a place of forgiveness. At its dedication in July 1990, the Archbishop of Tuam, Dr Joseph Cassidy, noted acurately in his address that it was a most unusual chapel:

> It doesn't stand up in the air as chapels usually do. It bows its head a bit, hunches its shoulders. It goes down on its knees, snuggles into the earth, prostrates itself before God in humility and self-effacement.

The chapel itself, in its very building and construction, speaks with the dispositions of those who enter it to lay aside their burdens and to come to reconciliation with God. By its very shape, form and design, it shows the attitudes called for in those who approach its doors seeking forgiveness and peace. If the chapel, as the archbishop describes it, is on its knees, prostrate before God in humility and self-effacement, this is because it is a chapel for sinners called to approach a merciful God in prayer, humility and self-effacement to receive the forgiveness of their sins.

Dr Cassidy pointed out on this occasion also that the chapel had been built in response to a need. The chapel had been made necessary because of 'the increasing number of pilgrims and the steady recourse to the Sacrament of Reconciliation'. And he added: 'People see their visit to Knock not just as a day out, but as a day out and back, a day for turning …'

Mgr Dominick Grealy, speaking on the same occasion, stressed particularly that without confessors and counsellors the building would be pointless and useless. He noted the fact that the chapel drew on the services of over two hundred priests from Tuam and other dioceses to assist in the ministry of sacramental reconciliation. He prayed:

> May this building be a source of healing of the countless wounds that afflict us all – physical, mental and spiritual. May it be a haven of peace, a rest for souls, a Chapel of Reconciliation with God and neighbour.

Each year, thousands of pilgrims avail of the Sacrament of Reconciliation at Knock. The Chapel of Reconciliation is the focal point, the goal of the journey for very many pilgrims who come to Knock. Many who have not received the sacrament for a long while, maybe years, find again through counselling and confession a greater peace of mind and contentment than they have known for a long time. As the archbishop remarked in his address at the dedication of the chapel:

> There is no more harrowing experience in life than to have to live with an accusing conscience. It poisons the mind, pervades the whole spirit, is seriously destructive of joy. There is a deep-seated need in the human heart for healing and forgiveness. I am happy to think that the troubled pilgrim will find that healing here.

And, looking to the future of the chapel, the archbishop added:

> I'm happy to think that millions of pilgrims can meet God's mercy in this chapel and that they can celebrate the Sacrament of Reconciliation in a spacious setting and in an atmosphere of tranquility and prayer.

CHAPTER 6

Life: Pilgrimage in Mystery

✠ *Michael Neary*

The 1979 oratory was replaced by the current Apparition Gable Chapel in 1992, with seating for 150 people.

Unless we are fortunate enough to be supported by a community of faith there is little in our culture to nurture a strong awareness of God. (Ruth Burrows: *Living in Mystery*, p 36).

The best starting point for a prayerful pilgrimage is an openness to seeing life as a mystery, as a place where God is actively present. We are made in the image of God, in the image of a creative God. We continue God's creative presence. 'We live before we learn how to live' (Lonergan). Life has questions to which we have no full answers. God is at work there, drawing us to himself. Mystery calls for wonder, for a sense of awe and reverence. This attitude does not come easily in a world that wants solutions, that seeks control of events. There is a desire to control through knowledge, through need for instant information and claiming the right to it, through seeking to be in charge of our destiny. Cardinal Martini asks the question, 'Why does God present himself to the world as the weak, despised, crucified one?' Pilgrimage can be a help to seeing life as the mystery that it is, whereas looking to false certainties can lead to elimination of the sense of mystery. All of life is a pilgrimage, a mystery of God leading, purifying, inspiring us, as we journey towards him.

To go on pilgrimage is to try and tune in with God's ways in us on our pilgrimage of life. The prayer of the pilgrimage opens us to the mystery of his presence, to patterns of his work. Prayer is unprotected existence. In it God wants to speak to us, to touch our pain points and heal us, to inspire our living with his truth, to draw us into wonder at his ways. We can resist seeing life as mystery and look on it as a problem to be solved. We can be in a hurry and resist the waiting that God wants of us in our efforts to understand what he is giving and asking. Loss of a sense of mystery leads to a diminished sense of sin (our great sin is ingratitude), to a diminished sense of self as a sinner in need of salvation from Jesus. A need of Jesus' mercy is an essential part of our relationship with him. Prayer on pilgrimage can lead to a rediscovery of ourselves as loved, redeemed sinners, as people called to deep gratitude for what Jesus has done and continues to do for us. Knock brings healing of many kinds. There can be a healing of anxiety through the gift of peace which prayer and togetherness in pilgrimage brings. There can be healing of the wounds of our past through fresh insight into the mercy and goodness of God. There can be healing of fears through the strength which we are given. A key moment in our healing is when we can allow brokenness (whatever it is for each of us personally) become an openness to God. Our world does not encourage such admission of fragility, though the reality of our fractured selves is obvious for all who want to see. We journey on in search of wholeness, of the healing of the fragmentation that sin brings. The purpose of a religious pilgrimage is to visit and worship at the place where a unique manifestation of divine activity has occurred, or where some particularly sacred memory is preserved. On pilgrimage there is an opportunity to put our lives into a new perspective, to become inserted more deeply into the plan of God. The struggle of other pilgrims and their faith in God's providential care is given to us as support and encouragement, as a way to allow God to lead each of us into his gift of peace.

Knock is a place of worship, an oasis of peace in a troubled world. History and mystery unite to make it possible for pilgrims to transcend the daily problems and pressures which weigh us down and dishearten us. When the apparition took place in 1879 the people of Ireland were just emerging from the devastation of the famine of 1845-1849. In the West the people had to cope with even more recent famine, in the mid eighteen sixties and the late eighteen seventies. Evictions were common place and led to the birth of the Land League.

The Lord hears their cry

The people were defenceless and dejected, poor, hungry and homeless, with very little sign of hope. In ancient Israel there was a group of people known as the Anawim – the poor of the Lord. These people recognised the fragile nature of life, their faith was in the Lord and they recognised that there was nowhere they could look for vindication so they put their trust in the Lord. This mentality finds expression in many of the Psalms. Our Lady was one of this group.

She gives expression to that faith in her Magnificat. This hymn acknowledges the Lord as the One who brings about the transformation of historically oppressive structures. It speaks of an economic revolution – 'hungry shall be filled with good things', a social revolution – 'he has put down the mighty from their thrones and exalted the lowly', and a moral revolution – 'he has scattered the proudhearted'. The people who lived at the time of the apparition could readily identify with these sentiments. Today all who look for hope beyond the human take comfort and solace from the way a merciful God intervenes on behalf of his people in need.

This has been the pattern of God's action throughout Israel's history. The people are suffering, they cry out to God who hears their cry and intervenes on their behalf. In their slavery the Israelites cry in complaint, calling for justice against their oppressors. Their call reaches God, the judge of human history who enters the scene to save the oppressed.

Penance

Penance is part of our sacred journey. There are times when we need to stop and ask whether we are being evangelised by a world that has a set of values that differ from those of the gospel. What once we regarded as luxuries may be seen now as necessities. The world we live in is both grace-bearing and grace-resisting. There are moments when it is opportune to pause and reflect on how the prevailing culture is either furthering our goal as Christians or hindering us in making progress on our pilgrimage. True fulfilment and sacrifice are in fact inseparable. The goal of our penance, as of our pilgrimage, is a right relationship with God, our giving to him what he is asking. Ruth Burrows says our greatest renunciation may be that of letting go of self pity and choosing to be happy in a world of limitations. That renunciation entails listening to God, allowing him to show us where we have failed in our response to his goodness. This means letting him heal our blindness to the truth, the blindness which is the result of sin. Our sin is often our self-sufficiency, the pride that wants to make us the centre of life. We would like to be able to heal ourselves, to cure ourselves, at times even to be independent of God. Because we sometimes forget, take for granted the gifts of God and thus become superficial in our living, we need to repent and remember what God has done, what he has given. Pilgrimage is a time to recall, to notice, to make sure we are choosing life in the decisions we take. The word of God reminds us that all is a gift (Rom 3; Eph 2:9-10). The challenge, then, is to receive it as gift. God is love (1 Jn 4:8); can I let him be love for me? God wants my surrender to him, but can I let go of control? A real wonder at God's gifts can lead to a truly profound repentance, a true coming home to him.

The cross

The cross and the lamb are closely related in the depiction of the apparition. The cross is the instrument by which Jesus liberated us from the power of sin. Jesus had reminded us that unless we take up our cross daily and follow him we cannot be his disciples. The cross is a real experience for each of us. It takes different forms, advancing age, ill-health, worry about examinations, about employment, concern about troublesome relationships, coping with one's own limitations. The cross can leave us sour and disgruntled or it can serve to make us aware of our need for help – the help of the Lord and support of others. In this way the cross serves to open up the self to new possibilities. Pilgrims carry their different crosses with them to Knock.

The Eucharist

The arrival point of Israel's pilgrimages was the place of God's presence in Jerusalem. Jesus' pilgrimage to Jerusalem culminated with his arrival in his Father's house. The high point of our pilgrimage is our meeting with the presence of the Lord in the Eucharist. Put simply, what we celebrate there is that God is great. The Eucharist calls our attention to the transforming action of God. He who transforms the bread and wine is actively transforming our hearts, healing, purifying, strengthening us. He wants us to notice his gifts and respond in gratitude. In the Eucharist our prayer is one of wonder and with that wonder we touch life in depth. We give thanks to God for his plan, for his ways which are different from ours. Our prayer takes on the features of Jesus' prayer (Lk 10:21). The Eucharist is a prayer of surrender as we entrust ourselves into God's plan, saying our 'yes' to his work in us. In the Eucharist we celebrate his healing presence. We hear his good news which heals our memories of the bad news we are exposed to in our daily existence. We remember with joy the wonder of our progressive transformation by our saving God. There we recall our identity as 'an everlasting gift' to the Father. Thanksgiving and praise are our finest response to the God who is great. Our primary relationship is with him and that relationship gives shape to all other relationships in our lives.

Liturgy is not a resting place. God sends us out in peace from prayer to share his gifts with others. From the Eucharist we are sent back into the midst of life so that we can be Christ for others, so that the healing and peace we have found may become gifts for the whole church. God invites us to be inserted into the struggle for justice in the world, to be active in pushing back the forces of darkness and fear. The sharing of the Eucharist is a call to responsibility for those who have no bread, no peace, no relationship with the God of mercy.

The family

One of the most beautiful sights during pilgrimages to Knock is to see the family, the three generations, some being carried in the arms, others linked or pushed in wheelchairs on their pilgrim path. The apparition at Knock has a strong familial character. When Our Lady came she brought her family with her, Jesus in the person of the Lamb, and St Joseph. Does this not say something to us today of the value of the family going on pilgrimages as a family?

In St John's gospel a new community is born at the cross on the occasion of the death of Jesus. With the words to Our Lady, 'this is your son', and the words to the beloved disciple, 'this is your mother', Jesus inaugurates the new community. Tradition has it that the beloved disciple is probably St John the Evangelist. If that is so then we have the wider family of the church represented in the apparition. Perhaps this accounts for the attraction which Knock has for families on pilgrimage.

In the Apparition Chapel at Knock it's the crowd at the altar which sparks off a rich vein of thought. At other shrines, it is the single statue of Mary which will focus the attention. That is not so here.

At Knock, the story of family sacrifice can be read in the eyes and on the hands of the pilgrim men and women who crowd here on sunny summer Sundays or come quietly when the weather is less friendly. These the men and women whose hands are marked and lined by lives of sacrifice and giving.

There are mothers here whose unsung unobtrusive self-giving and sacrifices made sons and daughters inherit a fuller and more challenging life than they ever knew. There is what one writer called the white martyrdom of so many mothers who swallowed their disappointments and concealed their broken hearts as they spent themselves in a lifetime of caring and nurturing children.

Pilgrimage and the contemporary culture

The contemporary culture tends to encourage a very utilitarian approach to God, to people and to the created world. God is frequently approached as the last resort when all else fails, people are valued for productivity and profit rather than as persons, while the created world is forced into ever greater production and yields.

The non-utilitarian relationship is expressed in worship. There God is adored, people are respected as made in his image and nature is seen as God's creation. Worship takes the focus and the pressure off ourselves and contemplates God as the centre. In this way we receive a new insight into ourselves as did the psalmist: 'When I look at the heavens, the work of your hands, the moons and stars which you have made; what is man that you are mindful of him, the son of man that you care for him?'

Prayer and pilgrimage

Knock was an obscure West of Ireland village until Our Lady appeared in 1879. Pilgrims today include all nationalities, classes and ages, the sick being particularly prominent.

Prayer is a constant at the shrine. This prayer may be full of confidence, or weakened by doubt and vacillation; it may be simple as that of a child, or virile and direct as the prayer of a grown person, hesitant upon the lips of an atheist or unbeliever, but piercing the clouds when uttered by a mother who is prepared to implore the gift of heaven. It may be the calm and submissive prayer of a soul already cleansed by suffering, or the heroic prayer of the patient who offers herself/himself up as a sacrifice for the benefit of someone else. People come carrying crosses of bereavement, sickness whether in themselves or in the family, worry and concern about the family, about the future, about unemployment and emigration.

We all have sacred places in our memories. It may be the place we first met our spouse, the chapel in which people got married, were professed or ordained. Knock is a sacred place where the veil between heaven and earth was drawn aside. In this place earth unites with heaven as graces and blessings are available to the pilgrim.

People on pilgrimage have a common purpose. Prayer does not cause them embarrassment. They have no inhibitions about the way people show their faith in God and their love for the mother of God. They may not express it in this way but they are involved in a search for eternal truth.

Pilgrims – disorientation – searching

There are times in life when everything seems to be going according to plan. There's a sense of being at home with oneself, a time characterised by absence of tension, a feeling of fulfilment. We may, even briefly, have had the experience of having put it all together, of having come to a good understanding of God and of coping well with life. Human relationships are not troublesome. We are undisturbed and uncritical. Prayer at a time like that is a joy. The orderliness, goodness and reliability of life call for a celebration of the status quo.

Then something happens to turn that controlled world upside down and inside out. It may be sickness, death of a dear one, disappointment or failure. There's a deep reluctance to let go of a world that has passed away and related to this is the reluctance to face up to the new situation. Any pilgrim at Knock prays at sometime for a new beginning, new vitality and new life.

The dislocation and disorientation is a dangerous and difficult time, a time when the sky is about to fall; the pieces which dovetailed so beautifully and with such little effort are now seen to have jagged edges. God, prayer, human relationships all carry huge question marks. Like the psalmist we cry 'out of the depths'. We are driven to the extremities of emotion. We find it difficult to speak about such experiences; we feel there is no safe reality about which we may speak. We become deeply aware of the disparity and distance between appearance and reality. We struggle against such situations with all our energies. It's a time of testing of nerve and patience. We are inclined to look back, to grasp for old certainties, to wish for them and to deny they are gone. We are conscious of the present as a very lean time.

A new movement of reorientation comes through the new situation. It comes as a surprise and we don't expect to be surprised. In this new movement, which comes as a gift from God, we discover something which is genuinely new and not just a repetition of the old. We begin to experience that the world has coherence; devastating hopelessness is not the final answer. We realise that the waters will not drown; we become conscious of the fact that the tomb which was sealed is empty. We realise that we must not forever lament, complain, protest and question. There's a time for affirmation and rejoicing, a time to end the criticism and to receive the gift of the new. The new movement of reorientation comes when, with the help of God, we begin to put the pieces together again in a new way, this time in his way – this time with God at the centre.

In its own unique way, all of creation offers its praise to God. What God wants of his people is an acknowledgement of him that flowers in worship, in praise and gratitude. That movement of praise is always going on among his people. As a pilgrim people we are invited to draw others into that movement of wonder and reverence so that an authentic prayer of praise is given to God. People have a right to know how much they are loved by God, and who is this God who loves them. On their pilgrim journey they need shepherds to guide them, to protect and heal them. A pilgrimage which heightens alertness to the shepherding care of God, coming directly and through others who mirror his care (nurses, doctors who care for the sick), strengthens his people for the task of being shepherds to one another. Those who have met the generosity of God on their own journey will want to be generous with others. They will want to share. Through this sharing they express their praise of God in action. 'Those who are certain about the last things can be at peace when dealing with the second last things' (Guardini).

The Contributors

TOM NEARY, a secondary teacher, is Chief Steward at Knock Shrine and is author of numerous books on the subject.

DONAL FLANAGAN is a theologian and journalist.

CHRISTOPHER O'DONNELL, O. CARM., teaches theology at Milltown Institute in Dublin.

MICHAEL DRUMM is a priest of the Diocese of Elphin. He teaches at Mater Dei Institute in Dublin.

SR ANGELA FORDE is Director of the Knock Counselling Service.

DR MICHAEL NEARY is Archbishop of Tuam.